THIS IS IT... THE FIRST B
THE STRC

Copyright © 2003 Omnibus Press
(A Division of Music Sales Limited)

Cover & book designed by Fresh Lemon.
Picture research by Dave Brolan & Julie Barber.

ISBN: 0.7119.9601.6
Order No: OP49159

Exclusive Distributors:
Music Sales Limited,
8/9 Frith Street, London W1D 3JB, UK.

Music Sales Corporation,
257 Park Avenue South, New York, NY 10010, USA.

Macmillan Distribution Services,
53 Park West Drive, Derrimut, Vic 3030, Australia.

To the Music Trade only:
Music Sales Limited,
8/9 Frith Street, London W1D 3JB, UK.

Photo credits:
All LFI except Frank Spooner Pictures (10), PA/Pol Foto (11),
Jørgan Angel (16t), Star File (29, 35 & 88), Angela Lubrano (30, 64 & 69),
George Bodnar (39) & Daniel Coston/Retna (46).
Colour section: Rex Features (1), LFI (2/3), Kevin Winter/Image Direct (3),
Phil Knott/Camera Press (4/5, 8),
Steve Gillett (6, 7) & Tina McClelland (6/7).

Every effort has been made to trace the copyright holders of the
photographs in this book but one or two were unreachable.
We would be grateful if the photographers concerned would contact us.

Printed in Spain.

A catalogue record for this book is available from the British Library.

Visit Omnibus Press at www.omnibuspress.com

THIS IS IT... THE FIRST BIOGRAPHY OF

THE STROKES

MARTIN ROACH

OMNIBUS PRESS
London · New York · Sydney

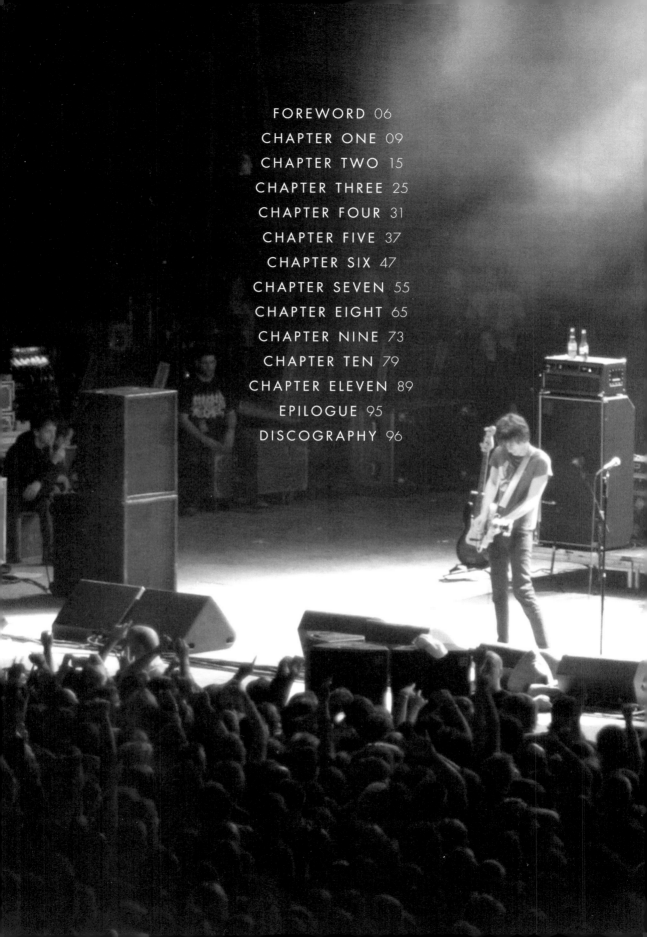

FOREWORD

THE Strokes. You already know the score. They're the best band on the planet. They are the saviours of rock'n'roll. Noel Gallagher loves them. So do supermodels and fashion designers. They only exist on the pages of *NME* and style mags while tickets for their shows are available exclusively to journalists and photographers. Born multi-millionaires, they buy radio airplay and profess to have written their songs when in fact they simply hire the best songwriters in the business with their rich parents' money. Styled by Calvin Klein, they often moonlight as catwalk models. Julian's business mogul father manages them. They're straight, gay, homophobic, homosexual. They drink too much but are strictly teetotal. They fight like streetcats but are actually achingly gentle. They are in love with themselves... and each other.

The Strokes are the inevitable result of an exponentially accelerating media culture. This is a band whose press profile, in the UK at least, has been constantly incongruous with their actual musical output and portfolio. Yet, on a grey day in August, 2002, The Strokes found themselves belting out their modestly brief set to an audience of 50,000 festival freaks on Reading's main stage. This headline slot – an honour shared that weekend with hard dance ubermeisters The Prodigy, an ecstatically received albeit mutated version of rock legends Guns N' Roses and Dave Grohl's Foo Fighters – came less than three years after The Strokes played their first ever show in a squalid, backstreet New York club in front of just six people.

Even by the fickle standards of twentieth century pop, this counts as a meteoric rise to fame, especially for a band cast in direct opposition to the Pop Idol mould. How that success came about is a strange collision of personalities, upbringings, application, coincidence and brutal, incendiary rock'n'roll.

CHAPTER ONE

"I DON'T KNOW FUCK ABOUT THE UNITED NATIONS. I'D RATHER SING ABOUT ROCK'N'ROLL AND CHICKS"

TOM PETTY

AMERICA and the rest of the world were in the grip of disco fever. The massive box office success of *Saturday Night Fever* had made John Travolta a genuine mega-star and simultaneously catapulted a resurgent Bee Gees to a new career pinnacle. The charts and the mainstream may have been crammed with gold lame, Boney M and glitter balls, but disco struggled to hide its seedy underbelly. August, 1978 saw New York's disco mecca Studio 54 being busted by undercover narcotics squad detectives posing as cocaine dealers. Delve further into the underground that same month and you would uncover the final days of a seminal New York new wavers, Television. Despite playing six sell-out shows at New York's Bottom Line club, their recent album, *Adventure*, had been poorly received by critics and their enigmatic and tempestuous four-year career ended amidst stories of heated inter-band clashes.

In the UK, punk was still frightening the establishment, although the rapidly fracturing Sex Pistols and the ultimate arrest of Sid Vicious for the murder of his girlfriend Nancy Spungeon offered confirmation that this most incendiary of all music genres was about to implode. Elsewhere in the world, Californian Congressman Leo Ryan was killed by the Reverend Jim Jones, who then successfully called for the cyanide suicide of nine hundred converts to his People's Temple cult (including himself, by gunshot), while the grisly exposure of the Khmer Rouge's genocide in Cambodia was fully realised. In July, 1978, Louise Brown, the world's first test tube baby, was born in England. A month later, a somewhat less medically pivotal birth came with the arrival in

New York of Julian Casablancas, on August 23, a birthday he shares with the dancer Gene Kelly and Who drummer Keith Moon, the wild man of British rock who had just 14 days left to live.

One of the regular taunts levelled at The Strokes is that they are little more than rich prep boys, born with silver spoons in their mouths and springboarded to success through wealth and privilege. Although the band have been at pains to explain otherwise, one rumour that swirled around the band was that Julian's father John managed them. Though he is undoubtedly a entrepreneur of no little skill, this is certainly not the case.

JULIAN'S FATHER, JOHN CASABLANCAS WITH TWO 'ELITE' MODELS, MIA ROSING (LEFT) AND TATIANA ROSSI

John Casablancas is the founder of the prestigious Elite Model Agency, home to a cluster of the world's highest paid supermodels. John had met Julian's mother – a Danish model and former Miss Denmark - while working in Paris and they were married shortly after. The couple relocated to New York where John set up Elite a year before Julian was born. By the time of Julian's arrival, Elite was already on the way to redefining how the model industry worked. With names such as Cindy Crawford, Linda Evangelista and Iman on the books, Elite was seen as the blueprint for a modern modelling agency, ushering in a new wave of corporate potential and media exposure previously unseen in the industry.

Julian's father cuts an imposing figure, standing at 6' 2" and boasting a worldwide reputation as a hugely successful and wealthy businessman. More recently, however, two Elite executives resigned in the wake of the BBC's *MacIntyre Undercover*, an investigative documentary highlighting some of the seedier aspects of the modelling industry. Elite declared it was "furious its reputation had been sullied by the off-duty remarks of a minority group within the organisation". John Casablancas himself was never implied or accused by the television show and is renowned as an unswerving advocate of declining to work with models who are known to use drugs. He is also famed for his scathing views on certain elements of the modelling world, most notably when he refused to continue working with tantrum-prone Naomi Campbell. He also called Heidi Klum "a German sausage".

Surely, The Strokes' naysayers protest, a contact as powerful and wealthy as John Casablancas must have been harvested for the nepotistic benefit of the band, particularly in light of their uncharitable reputation in some circles as transparent fashionistas. Not so. Julian's father was estranged from his mother when

JULIAN'S MOTHER
JEANETTE CHRISTJANSEN
FORMER MISS DENMARK

The Strokes' frontman was only seven and henceforth they saw each other only occasionally. When Julian did visit his father, the emotional bond was inevitably somewhat strained. "When I visited him it was a little fucking strange… your dad has this lifestyle that seems kind of cool but, at the same time, you're sort of not getting along and you don't really want to see him."

Dipping his teenage toe into his father's glamorous world did not attract Julian. At one point, his father was dating supermodel Stephanie Seymour, future girlfriend of Guns N' Roses frontman Axl Rose. In 1994, John was married for the third time, to a 17-year-old Brazilian called Aline Wermelinger, whom he met at a modelling contest staged by Elite. Asked later if his father might have been behind the use of Strokes' songs on the catwalks of Milan and Paris, Julian simply said, "I doubt it".

"MY MUM WAS FUCKING MISERABLE AND I JUST LIVED WITH HER CRYING EVERY DAY"

After Julian's parents had split up, he was raised by his mother in New York. In the immediate aftermath of the marital breakdown, the young Julian found life very difficult: "My mum was fucking miserable and I just lived with her crying every day." He later intimated to *The Face* that trying to cope with the emotional upset of his mother provided his first real experience of depression: "When you feel serious pain and serious depression in your life… your fists clench and you have to do something or you're just going to kill yourself." He has also explained that his natural inclination is to think in depth all the time and this pensive aspect of his personality can make him prone to bouts on undue solemnity.

Julian speaks Danish and Spanish but his early educational career was not impressive. In his pre-teens, he was by his own admission, "fucking up in school". For some time he had been the class clown, always fooling around, but the negative consequences for his schoolwork were offset by the effect this comic persona had on his desirability to the opposite sex. With a sullen coolness that would later stand him in perfect stead for fronting The Strokes, he started to withdraw and appear aloof. He also enjoyed his first taste of alcohol at an unusually early age, craftily slurping the final few mouthfuls from spent glasses during a party at his father's house. For a while, he took to drinking quite often and, after being caught with alcohol one day by the school authorities, he was ordered to attend a state 'rehab' facility called Phoenix House twice a week.

LE ROSEY

Established 1880

Concerned that such errant behaviour would damage his educational prospects, John's parents sent him to an ultra-exclusive finishing school in Switzerland when he was 13.

Established in 1880, L'Institut Le Rosey was one of the world's oldest private schools, and Julian's father had himself been a student there. Most pupils were the children of super-rich Europeans or Middle East families, embroiled who could afford to shell out £10,000 a term for the privilege of attending.

The school's austere code of discipline was seen as the ideal way to iron out Julian's more extravagant edges. Predictably, this clashed like oil and water with his independent spirit. When he was found smoking one day, he was sent for the first of many cross-country dawn runs across the frozen, snow-covered school grounds.

Julian usually expresses a total revulsion for his time at Le Rosey, saying mainly that it was "very, very weird". In *NME*, he was rather more graphic, recalling with distaste how… "it sucked. There were a lot of Turkish people there. They were nice, but you know… they all wore Versace jeans. It was the biggest culture shock of my life." He hated all of his teachers and spent all term craving the final day of school. When his fellow classmates headed out for the weekly shopping trips to designer boutiques, Julian locked himself in his room in splendid isolation. Julian later reversed, or at least reconsidered, his opinions, telling *NME* that "it was a nice place. I have good memories and some less good memories."

Although Le Rosey has vehemently denied rumours that Osama Bin Laden was once a pupil there, it is a fact that Ben Gautrey of the Cooper Temple Clause attended when he was just six. Such celebrity association was ironically the root of the eventual watershed effect this conservative establishment would have on Julian's life - it was here he met fellow student and future Strokes colleague Albert Hammond.

ALBERT HAMMOND

CHAPTER TWO

"GRUNGE IS WHAT HAPPENS WHEN CHILDREN OF DIVORCE GET THEIR HANDS ON GUITARS"

NEWSWEEK

ALTHOUGH Albert stayed at Le Rosey for only six months, in that short time he and Julian struck up a lasting friendship. As the only two Americans at the school, the pair were naturally drawn to each other. Albert was seven months younger than Julian, having been born in Los Angeles in April, 1979. He came from a musical family, with a British-born father and Argentinian mother, the daughter of a diplomat. His father, Albert Hammond Senior, was raised in Gibraltar and enjoyed a career as a noted singer and songwriter. His first major success was co-authoring 'Little Arrows' for Leapy Lee with Mike Hazelwood and a year later the pair penned 'The Air That I Breathe', an international hit for The Hollies. In 1972 Hammond enjoyed a big hit in his own name with the soft rock anthem 'It Never Rains In Southern California' and, two years later in the UK, with 'Free Electric Band'. With Carole Bayer Sager he wrote Leo Sayer's 1977 UK number one 'When I Need You', and he has since written tunes for Art Garfunkel, Celine Dion, Julio Iglesias and Chicago. His son Albert picked up his first guitar at the age of nine.

At this point, Julian could not even play an instrument and had little knowledge of music. That was all about to change. His mother had recently met and married Sam Adoquei, whom Julian credits with introducing him to music in the very first instance. Sam sent a package to Julian in Switzerland containing the album *The Best Of The Doors*. The quartet led by Jim Morrison had an immediate and profound impact on the unsettled teenager: "That night I stayed in my room and just played it over and over again. I listened really intensely to every instrument, to every word, to the way the choruses fit and then - poof! - it all fell into place... I knew then how music was built." Back in New York between terms, Sam and Julian would often talk for hours about art, music, performance. Sam augmented Julian's growing interest in anything to do with music with some home truths about stardom, explaining just how gruelling and demanding the lifestyle can be. Such formative advice and fascinating conversations left a profound mark on the young Julian's mind.

ALBERT HAMMOND SENIOR

Whatever interest in academia Julian might once have entertained was not revitalised by his stay at Le Rosey. His mother noticed her son becoming increasingly withdrawn and decided to bring him back him to the Big Apple to attend the equally exclusive Dwight School on Manhattan's Upper West Side. Prestigious Dwight alumni included author Truman Capote, pop artist Roy Lichtenstein and former New York mayor Fiorello La Guardia, after whom the airport was named. The problem of Julian's increasing insularity was not remedied at Dwight where he was only marginally less isolated than at Le Rosey. In the school cliques and in-crowds, Julian was the perpetual outsider, an unlikely tag in light of The Strokes future super-cool status, but for now he gravitated towards two other similarly unorthodox pupils (and future Strokes cohorts), Nick Valensi and Fab Moretti.

Nick Valensi was born in New York on January 16, 1981. The town was then in mourning for John Lennon, whose murder on the city streets by deluded fan Mark Chapman had occurred the

NICK VALENSI

previous month. Nick's father is Tunisian and his mother French. He first played guitar aged five.

Fabrizio was born in Rio De Janeiro, Brazil at a time when the country's Amazonian region was the scene of a lawless gold rush by 25,000 prospectors who eventually unearthed $50 million worth of nuggets. The rush brought desperately needed income to a country which at that time had the largest foreign debt in the world. Fabrizio's Italian father enjoyed a more comfortable life than the majority of the population, playing guitar on cruise ships sailing in the oceans off South America. When Fabrizio was just three years old, his parents emigrated to New York, and soon after bought him a drum kit. They had not wasted their money – the young Fab practised constantly inside a soundproofed closet in his mother's house. A doomed spell as an altar boy was quickly replaced by Guns 'N' Roses and Bob Marley albums.

"IT'S NOT LIKE WE'RE POSH KIDS OR ANYTHING... WE ALL STILL HUNG OUT ON THE STREET AND DRANK 40S"

FAB MORETTI

The Dwight School was not quite as exclusive as Le Rosey, but neither was it a hotbed of inner-city angst and dysfunctional children attending school soely to escape from their desperately poor home life. Julian agrees, but is quick to defend himself against accusations of privilege, telling *The Face* magazine: "It's not like we're posh kids who drove fancy cars or anything. You've got to have money to live in Manhattan, but we all still hung out on the street and drank 40s." Unavoidably perhaps, such apparent childhood elitism fuels much of the cynicism aimed at The Strokes.

Of course, this criticism holds water only if you accept the dubious school of thought that says only tortured bedsit artists existing on crumbs and tap water can produce great music, or indeed, great art. Which is obviously bunkum. John Lydon famously asserted that rock'n'roll was a working-class pursuit and coming from the viewpoint of punk rock, there is a clear element of truth in that. Agreed, it might sound shallow singing about bringing down the government and fighting poverty if your parents' income is in seven figures, but The Strokes have never claimed to be The Levellers or Rage Against The Machine. Furthermore, music history is littered with countless essential artists to whom poverty was a stranger. Radiohead are highly educated men from middle-class backgrounds, yet Thom Yorke has rightly established himself as one of the world's most emotive artists in rock, often scouring the darkest of themes for his enigmatic work. Queen's Freddie Mercury came from a well-to-do, though subsequently impoverished, family from Zanzibar but that did not stifle, or indeed, invalidate his creative muse. Bob Dylan's father owned a furniture and electrical store, but this decidedly middle-class background doesn't mean Dylan has no right to his reputation as one of the greatest singer-songwriters of all-time. What about Pete Townshend, whose dad was a successful saxophone player? Or John Lennon, whose surrogate mum Aunt Mimi certainly aspired to become middle-class? The list goes on. Money or privilege and artistic creativity are not mutually exclusive, period.

AFTER leaving Le Rosey, Julian discovered his first musical love in the underground noise emanating from Seattle in the late Eighties and early Nineties – grunge. Prior to the Nineties, Seattle had no musical identity to call its own. It could claim Jimi Hendrix amongst its alumni, and there were other successes such as The Sonics, The Fleetwoods, and several more mainstream artists such as Robert Cray, Heart, Kenny G, Quincy Jones and Queensryche, but these successes were sporadic and isolated, with no thread of association between them.

However, as the Eighties drew on, an underground scene was developing in the cold, north western corner of the United States that would turn the global mainstream on its head. Grunge emerged when a disparate group of bands started gigging relentlessly on the underground circuit, taking their cue from the dispossessed, 'slacker' generation of American kids who turned up to watch them. They sang about the aimless of life around them and they dressed in anti-fashion: shapeless check workshirts over torn jeans with lank, uncombed hair. Local label Sub Pop was at very nucleus of the scene, releasing a seminal series of limited edition records, including classic tracks by bands such as Sonic Youth, Steve Fisk, The U-Men, Skinny Puppy, Nirvana, and the often overlooked Green River.

There were hordes of other bands producing alternative music of note in this period. There was the quite brilliant Tad, Mudhoney, The Screaming Trees – these and many others released music that, to the youth of the day at least, was revolutionary. Older bands like The Melvins and Sonic Youth also enjoyed rejuvenated careers in the wake of numerous citations from the younger bands they had influenced. Detractors derided grunge's fusion of hardcore and metal as merely re-hashing Seventies rock, but this mattered little to those experiencing the music for the first time. For those in the thick of it, it felt like they were living through something important. Besides, the scuzzy, furious energy of grunge was rooted as much in the post-punk barrage of US hardcore bands like Black Flag (who were themselves compared to Led Zeppelin). Also, there was a clear lineage back to Sixties garage bands like The Sonics, MC5, The Stooges and The Kingsmen.

NIRVANA'S KURT KOBAIN

Like all subcultures and musical movements, this latest development was tagged only after it had already been around for some time (indeed, the term grunge itself was originally a tongue-in-cheek name). By then Nirvana had gone global with their ten million-selling album *Nevermind*, which single-handedly changed the face of modern music programming, live shows, record store buying policies and just about every facet of the music and entertainment industries. For example, in the wake of 'Smells Like Teen Spirit', MTV's aesthetic was virtually transformed overnight, ditching the bikini-clad babes of a thousand soft porn metal videos and replacing them with grunge's gritier, cheaper look. For the next two years, grunge ruled the world.

With the music came the culture – grunge, like punk before it, was truly thrift store chic. Bedecked in flannel shirts, oversized shorts cut off just below the knee and long, lank hair, the grunge kid quickly picked up the tag of 'loser'. Girls often wore flowery dresses with thick leggings, or trousers with oversized band T-shirts. It is strange that The Strokes seem to have picked up nothing – apart from perhaps a pair of Converse and the odd loose shirt – from the style of loser culture.

Unfortunately, as with so many subcultures, once grunge entered the mainstream it was effectively rendered culturally impotent by its own success. Nirvana's debut album *Bleach* was produced for just $606.17 – yet cheque book-waving A&R men were soon jetting into Seattle to throw six figure deals at almost anyone who looked like they could be the offspring of Neil Young. Some of these gambles paid off with multi-million selling albums, but many bands never achieved what they promised, unprepared as they were for the intense heat of the media spotlight.

"THE MOST POWERFUL ASPECT OF MUSIC IS TO GO ON WITH THE IDEAL THAT YOU CAN MAKE IT BETTER IF YOU DO YOUR THING"

Million dollar-marketing campaigns backed all the latest 'grungers', while cheesy TV shows ran features on what to say to your 'loser' teenager. Elevator music albums were released with muzak versions of grunge classics, and perhaps worst of all, haute couture designers started to copy the style. Milan and Paris catwalks exhibited horrendous copies of the grunge look, with obscenely priced and hideously shaped versions of thrift store chic. Record stores reported fashion journalists, dripping in designer garments, running in and asking for albums by grunge bands. Some even tried to re-title the designer wear 'frunge'. Lumberjack shirts with designers names were selling for over $500 and a corduroy jacket, virtually identical to thousands of second-hand coats worn by grunge fans, was offered for sale for $3,000.

And then of course, it all came to a screeching halt with the shot that was heard across the world, when Kurt Cobain committed suicide in early April 1994. His death effectively put an end to grunge, although for many it had

EDDIE VEDDER - PEARL JAM

already become passé after the corporate hijack, the familiar drug problems and the increasingly feeble music. In the vacuum left by Cobain's death, the grunge movement splintered and stumbled. Fortunately, in America, bands like Green Day and Offspring filled the void with their post-punk energy, and were met with multi-million sales, as there still seemed to be a thirst for the punk ethos.

Julian has made no secret of the fact that Pearl Jam were one of the first bands to quicken his pulse, in particular the track 'Yellow Ledbetter'. Eddie Vedder's group had followed Nirvana out of the grunge traps and were often unfairly criticised for taking what was perceived as a corporate approach, when in fact they strived constantly to confront the commerciality of the music world (keeping ticket prices low and refusing to record videos, for example). Nonetheless, Pearl Jam was one of few bands to emerge from the fallout of grunge with a genuinely lengthy career. Eddie Vedder and cohorts repeatedly fought the corporate record business with a variety of formats, releases and special concerts, but their efforts to strip back their music to its emotional core and purpose often merely cost them sales and sometimes popularity. Vedder's tortured vocals and bluntly frank lyrics proved to be the band's secret weapon, catapulting them to multi-million sales, at one point including the two fastest selling album ever in *Versus* and *Vitalogy*. On sales terms alone, they remain the biggest US rock band of the Nineties.

Pearl Jam and Nirvana delivered a musical expression of youthful angst that certainly impressed Julian. Although Pearl Jam and Nirvana are not as obvious as some of the bands to which The Strokes have been compared, they did make him think differently about music: "The most powerful aspect of music is the fact that it can open your eyes to the frustration of everything and give you the adrenaline and faith to go on with the ideal that you can make it better if you do your thing."

When Julian strummed a guitar for the first time, he picked out the bass line to Nirvana's 'Polly'. The intensity of grunge showed the fledgling songwriter that his own angst might somehow be reflected in song. He started to imagine being in a band and even admits to staging mock pop star interviews in his shower. At this time, Nick was taking extra guitar lessons at Dwight and shared a common love of grunge with Julian. Fab was also a fan.

Since leaving Le Rosey, Julian had been intent on forming a band, but found that few of his friends were interested in the rock records he relished, favouring instead hip hop and gangsta rap. It was a barren time looking for those who worshipped Lizard King Jim Morrison but the trio of Julian, Fab and Nick started to hang out together.

Fab was quite taken with Julian's presence from the first time they were around music together: "I was jamming with Nick and a guy called Danny," he recalled in *Blender* magazine, "and Julian came to visit. He just stayed and listened, didn't even play, but it was a rare old time. He was eating tacos, I believe." Julian didn't play an instrument that day because at that point he couldn't, but he soaked up the atmosphere of the ramshackle studio, the ambience of the equipment and the camaraderie of the musicians.

Soon, the three started going to gigs together. Although they had no defined goals at this stage, they just knew they wanted to be out there, listening to music, playing music, talking about music. Julian started to study musical composition at Five Towns College on Long Island. During the first few weeks of attending, Julian was out with a group of his new college mates when they invited him to a room and shut the door behind them. They stood in front of him and asked him to say his name, announce that he wanted to join their fraternity and then declare his favourite sexual position. Somewhat surprised, Julian said, 'My name is Julian Casablancas, I don't want to join your fraternity and I don't know why I am here." This incident perhaps sums up Julian's time at school, and reinforced his desire to hang out with kids like Fab and Nick.

The trio were soon augmented by Julian's lifelong friend, Nikolai Fraiture who had been to the same elementary school as The Strokes' singer. "Everything we went through for the first time together, your first cigarette,

your first drink." Nikolai was also born in New York, on November 13, 1978, to French and Russian parentage. He schooled at Le C'est Francais and is consequently bilingual. Like Fabrizio, an early spell as an altar boy gave him an early musicality but he was asked to leave after trying to impress the girls too much. He was the quietest of the four friends.

Nikolai played bass, so inevitably the foursome started jamming together and forming ideas for a band. Calling themselves Half Pipe, a ramshackle 'gig' was even played at a 21st birthday party thrown by Nick's older sister, in front of a gaggle of girls.

NICKOLAI FRAITURE

CHAPTER THREE

"SOMEBODY SAID TO ME THAT THE BEATLES WERE ANTI-MATERIALISTIC. THAT'S A HUGE MYTH. JOHN AND I LITERALLY USED TO SIT DOWN AND SAY, 'NOW, LET'S WRITE A SWIMMING POOL'"

PAUL McCARTNEY

THE fifth and final piece of the Strokes' jigsaw fell into place in the autumn of 1998. Albert Hammond Junior, Julian's friend from Le Rosey had been living in Los Angeles but decided to head east and resurfaced in New York, ostensibly to attend NYU film school. Once there, he looked up his old school friend Julian, inadvertently landing himself a role in one of the most talked about bands of the new Millennium.

Julian told Albert about his three friends and their ad hoc band. He also explained that although the four were very close, the musical chemistry was not quite right and that they were considering auditioning for a second guitarist. Julian himself preferred to just sing and was deeply uncomfortable playing second guitar. Albert felt this was the perfect moment to reveal his hobby. He'd played guitar in a few short-lived groups in Los Angeles, but had been kicked out of his last band because the singer felt he would be unable to perform on stage. Julian was delighted and asked Albert to attend a jamming session the very next day. He was recruited on the spot.

The arrival of Hammond provided the musical and emotional catalyst around which the Strokes' line-up coalesced. Prior to his arrival they were just "four people making bad music". As Nick explained, "before Albert joined, we sucked. It wasn't easy. My mom was strict and didn't want me to spend all my time playing music. I was kind of pessimistic we'd ever find the right dude… (but) after Albert came in, it slowly became something decent. Then it became something good. And now it's on its way to being something great."

Yet Albert modestly claims he didn't really start playing guitar intensely until he met the rest of the band. He had a mastery of the basic bar chords and scales but did not class himself as adept. He even goes as far to suggest the other band members had to cajole him into improving: "I got kicked in the ass a lot by the others... 'You gotta practice more, you're not good enough yet...' And that hurt, man, but healthy criticism was what made this band tight."

With their gang now solidified, The Strokes started to scurry around New York's underground, attending gigs by artists such as Guided By Voices, the Reverend Horton Heat and The Mooney Suzuki. Back at their digs they would sit up into the small hours playing Bob Marley, Velvet Underground and obscure grunge B-sides. From the very start, the five friends were inseparable, going to every gig, every party, everywhere. This was their musical apprenticeship, soaking up past and present influences, formulating their sound, establishing their musical lineage.

"WE WERE TRYING TO DO SOMETHING INTERESTING, BUT IT WAS NOT GOOD. IT WAS LIKE A ROUGH MOCK-UP"

Albert was anxious to hone his guitar skills, but the manner in which he stumbled across future teacher and Strokes 'guru' JP Bowersock is pure New York. He was walking around the streets of Manhattan trying to get his Rickenbacker 360 repaired when he was approached by "a weirdo" in the street. The man asked him if he used handmade strings and offered to sell him some. Albert went with a friend to this man's digs and was subsequently introduced to ex-policeman Richie Baxt, who sold guitars and equipment from his apartment and was very well connected on the New York scene. Crammed into his tiny flat were dozens of guitars and mountains of equipment, squashing his small bed into a corner of the room. The five friends would regularly go round to Richie's and hang out, play guitars and talk about music, while Richie would repair their guitars or recommend new ones. He was the cheapest in New York and The Strokes have since bought all of their guitars from him.

Richie suggested Albert contact JP Bowersock for lessons. A big man nearing forty, complete with tousled moustache and triangular goatee, Bowersock was an imposing figure. Albert was so impressed with his first few sessions with JP that Julian was soon taking lessons as well, with his advice quickly expanding past just technical guitar tuition. JP spent a lot of time talking to Julian about the craft of songwriting, sharing ideas and brainstorming song concepts. Nick also started working with JP too. Albert later told *Guitar Magazine* how, "JP helped me discover (things) about music, like how to discover empty spaces. It wasn't this strict teacher thing. He showed me Freddie King, Link Wray for the balls, Elmore James." Very quickly, five fledgling Strokes' knowledge of the Seattle scene was hugely augmented by a comprehensive and expert take on music history.

The Strokes were officially christened as such in 1999, a few months before their début gig. Talking to *The Face* in August 2002, Fab explained their moniker in more depth: "We'd rejected a bunch of names. Nikolai said one that made us laugh for days, 'De Niros'. I used to think of what the word actually meant: a stroke (he holds his heart in an inaccurate medical mime), a stroke… blow to the face… a stroke in painting… but now I just think of five dudes standing around." Nikolai added, 'Then there's the obvious sexual undertones… it rolled off the tongue really well, sort of violent and sort of sexual, it just sounded cool to everyone."

Indicative of the band's deceptively diligent approach, The Strokes spent six hard months during the first half of 1999 rehearsing their sound in a tiny studio in the Hell's Kitchen district of Manhattan. The room in the Music Building cost $300 a month to rent, mostly financed by a variety of day jobs, including selling frozen yoghurt, working in a second-hand record store and bar work. Rock'n'roll this might be, but rehearsals were sacrosanct, beginning religiously at 10pm and continuing through the night until 8am. Madonna had previously rehearsed there and even graffiti-ed on the studio wall, while outside the walk home was something of a lottery which saw Nick mugged three times in the same night by the same man. Long nights of rehearsals dragged on forever, but each band member refused to run before they could walk. Eventually, The Strokes held a shared consensus that they were ready for their first public gig. It was September 1999.

"WE WATCHED *SPINAL TAP* AND LEARNED A LOT"

SEPTEMBER 14th, 1999 saw The Strokes' live premier at a dingy and now-defunct little club called The Spiral. Music legend holds that there were only six people present and the band knew four of them. Racked with nerves, Julian vomited before going on stage. For once, The Strokes' soon-to-be-legendary self-promotion was not on view: "We didn't want them to see us," said Julian. "We were trying to do something interesting, but it was not good. It was like a rough mock-up." Disappointed and demoralised by their performance, The Strokes hastily retreated to their rehearsal room to continue working on their songs. When they weren't in the rehearsal studio or in a bar talking about music, they were on the phone to each discussing their progress. Gradually, the surfaced, blinking into the hazy New York light, and started gigging again.

A spate of local 'toilet' venues hosted The Strokes' early shows. Several gigs were so off the beaten track that the promoter didn't even ask for a demo tape, a simple phone call requesting a slot was usually enough to earn a night's work. The Strokes displayed an admirable restraint in pacing their early career, happy to play at any venue, analysing each performance for hours after the show to find ways in which it could be improved. In true rock'n'roll tradition, the band inevitably played their share of nightmare early shows ("We watched *Spinal Tap* and learned a lot"). One particular band favourite was at a lobster restaurant in Delaware. The miniscule and cramped stage was bad enough but this was exacerbated by the virtually inoperable PA, which constantly cut out Julian's increasingly fractured vocals. To make matter worse, the band had only eight songs at this point, but at least the crowd – which consisted entirely of a family of five - didn't seem to mind.

Despite such knocks to their confidence, The Strokes were relentless in their self-promotion. They would hand out flyers for themselves at every available opportunity. When they went to gigs, sometimes three or four nights a week, they would flyer before and after the show. They stuck up posters where they could, talked to people on the scene about their band and generally worked tirelessly to complement the material they were practising relentlessly almost every day.

Their first real break came when they secured a slot at a more reputable, albeit still small gig, the Mercury Lounge on Manhattan's Lower East Side, just across the street from the scene of their first ever performance at The Spiral.

MANHATTAN'S MERCURY LOUNGE

CHAPTER FOUR

"I ALWAYS FELT THAT A LOT OF MY SONGS DEALT WITH SPYING ON MYSELF"

CARLY SIMON

AT such an early stage, The Strokes had only hastily-taped, very rudimentary home recordings of a few song ideas, but nothing with which they were entirely happy. They felt that in order to get quality gigs in and around New York, they needed a professional sounding demo. Beyond that, maybe such a demo might even win them a support slot on a national tour if they were lucky. So they all stopped their various college courses and began to work full time on the demo. As it turned out, what they produced during these brief recording sessions was a watershed recording which turned them into one of the most talked about bands on the planet.

The band chose to record their first serious demo at the Transporter Raum, owned by Gordon Raphael, a basement studio near the corner of Avenue A and 2nd Street in Manhattan's East Village. By comparison to the uninitiated Strokes, Raphael was a veritable music business veteran, having spent time touring as keyboardist with The Psychedelic Furs. After that he'd worked in his hometown Seattle with bands such as Green River and future members of Mudhoney. The Strokes knew nothing about his immersion in the early days of grunge when they first worked together, but it meant there was an immediate synergy and shared preference for a rudimentary approach to sound production. Raphael listed *Fragile* by Yes, *Electric Ladyland* by Jimi Hendrix, and *Flashes From The Archive Of Oblivion* by Roy Harper as his favourite three albums. After nearly twenty years of production duties, he had moved to New York in the hope of getting more work with European bands who visited the city; ironically, it was with a New York five piece that his name would enjoy fresh prominence.

Raphael had seen The Strokes play live alongside another New York band, Come On, only a few weeks before they walked into his studio to record their first demo. He has said that being "a small Manhattan studio owner, I have to hustle to keep my studio booked. I have to go to nightclubs to scout bands… I actually liked the other band, Come On, better."

The demo would contain no cover versions. The Strokes have cited Jimi Hendrix as one of the few artists who could make covers worthwhile by improving or altering the original to his individual style. Instead, they turned up at Raphael's studio clutching a trio of original songs ready to be committed to tape: 'The Modern Age', 'Last Nite' and 'Barely Legal'.

"I OFTEN HAVE THE URGE TO JUST GRAB ALL THE STRINGS AT THE SAME TIME, JUST 'COS I THINK IT SOUNDS COOL"

All The Strokes songwriting is credited to Julian alone. However, he is the first to acknowledge that the band's creative process is far more democratic than this suggests – which is why he splits the band's publishing earnings five ways. Julian will take a guitar line, a melody or a vocal idea into a rehearsal, where all five bandmates will work on the concept together to fruition. They claim that they never argue over songwriting and that Julian has never been didactic about his vision. The first recognisable Strokes song that was written in this way was 'Soma'.

WITH the help of Raphael's veteran production skills, The Strokes captured what has been described by some observers as one of the finest demo tapes ever recorded. Unlike, for example, U2's 'The Fly' which was also rumoured to have been a demo, this EP was brimming with raucous energy across all three songs, not just the lead track. The opener, 'The Modern Age', was a strangely melancholic yet riotous rant about the oddness of modern life. The song was drilled through with a stabbing guitar riff - the source of many future Velvet Underground comparisons - accompanied by a bruising drum line. Julian's voice was heavily distorted, sounding both like the studio couldn't afford decent microphones and yet as perfectly produced as any vocal could be. The overall effect was superb, bouncing from the staccato verse into the upbeat, singalong chorus with infectious abandon. Julian seemed to combine a streetwise cockiness with a refreshing innocence, a truly potent combination.

The opening guitar solo appends the first chorus, played brilliantly by Valensi as it descends hypnotically until it is almost imploding in on itself. This was a technically difficult guitar line, one which Nick enjoyed creating: "I like the idea of my shit collapsing. In the middle of a lead part, I often have the urge to take my hands off the fretboard, or just grab all the strings at the same time for no reason, just 'cos I think it sounds cool." The sudden arrival of the solo after the initial simple strumming takes the listener by surprise, and made many critics dive into their record collections for tracks by US garage forefathers The Stooges and MC5

The song then slams Julian into the next verse, as the drums thump on relentlessly while the tension tangibly builds, with Julian deftly guiding his naked vocal aggression to a compelling climax. The quickening pace of many Strokes songs recalls the motor-like drive of the Velvets and others, notably Television. Then, suddenly, it's all over, crashing to a close as the bass slides back out of earshot. Steeped in retro, achingly cool and ultra-modern. 'The Modern Age' demands the repeat button on the stereo.

Next up was another guitar driven blast with 'Last Nite', an even stronger track than the first song and certainly a landmark tune for The Strokes. Leaning more towards pop than the its predecessor's rock slant, this song had at its core a pseudo-reggae rhythm guitar that somehow hinted at a feelgood summer breeze. This time it was Albert's cunning guitar work that threw out various disjointed blues to add to the heady mix of abrasive fuzz noise. Nikolai's bass occasionally thumps out carefully placed and simple beats while Fab's thunderous, rock-steady drums sound as if they are actually in your living room. Again the distorted vocals, again the brief but memorable guitar solo, again an instant classic.

Closing the demo was 'Barely Legal'. With a much fuller sound than the previous two tracks, its more danceable drumming still sounded like it could have come from an Eighties drum machine. Retro riffing spliced through the song, although The Strokes mixed it up this time with softer guitar melodies. The result was oddly reminiscent of elements of Britpop mixed with Lou Reed (in a good mood). With the risqué subject matter and frantic delivery, this completed the demo superbly. When questioned on the meaning of this song's lyrics, Fab said: "It should be taken the way you interpret it. The lyrics mean different things to different people."

When the brief sessions for the demo were complete, Raphael was still not overwhelmed, saying, "I thought it was just a quick and dirty thing I would never hear about again."

I T was this demo tape that landed The Strokes the gig at The Mercury Lounge and, as a consequence, brought them to the attention of their future manager Ryan Gentles. Ryan was the venue's booker and prided himself on helping unsigned bands crawl up the ladder. His nouse for spotting worthy new bands mixed with this philanthropic attitude to the unsigned masses quickly earned the Mercury Lounge a solid reputation as a credible venue and an invaluable source of new talent. Its role in the New York music scene was akin to numerous A&R haunts in London's Camden.

"I'D GET A LOT OF THE SAME KIND OF SHIT IN THERE DAY AND DAY OUT"

A former musician himself, Gentles' almost endless patience with substandard rock acts often balked at the mountains of amateurish demo tapes which spilled onto his sagging desk every day. Fortunately, the sheer volume of submissions had not blunted his ear for talent, so when he first played The Strokes' tape it had a significant impact on him: "I'd get a lot of the same kind of shit in there day and day out," he recounted in *Penthouse* magazine. "When I got The Strokes demo, I was just so floored – out of all the submissions that came in, 20 or 30 a day, nothing ever stuck out like that. I actually took their tape home with me and played it over and over again for weeks."

Gentles himself was only a few years older than the young band. Being positioned so centrally in New York's club scene, he was perfectly qualified to recognise the slither of genius in his hands. He booked the band and watched their first show at the Mercury with growing excitement. Unbeknown to him, the début at the Mercury was equally memorable foe The Strokes: "That was like our dream place to play. It's the coolest small venue for local bands. Always in the back of our minds, we wanted to play the Mercury Lounge."

After the gig, Gentles made his admiration for The Strokes known to the band and offered to help them out on an informal basis. Within a matter of a few weeks, his phone was ringing off the hook with enquiries about them. Indeed, he was soon taking more calls about The Strokes than he was for booking enquiries at the Mercury, so out of courtesy to the venue, he quit and formed Wiz Kid Management. "If I hadn't quit, I would have been fired!"

CHAPTER FIVE

"I WAS SITTING IN A BAR THE OTHER DAY AND SOME GIRL SAID TO ME, 'DO PEOPLE ACTUALLY COME TO YOUR SHOWS OR IS IT JUST PEOPLE FROM MAGAZINES?'"

NICK VALENSI

WITH Ryan Gentles behind them, The Strokes career started to take off. Their new manager wasted no time in using his contacts and experience to land them opening slots on a national tour with Ohio's Guided By Voices and during a US visit by Mancunian media darlings The Doves, who were promoting their excellent *Lost Souls* album. The support gigs with Guided By Voices came about as a result of The Strokes' own fondness for band, together with an ingenious slice of guerrilla PR. Albert, Nick and Julian went to see them at Irving Plaza and threw a demo on stage – they were later amazed and delighted to find out that Guided By Voices loved their songs and had actually kept that tape for their tour bus. This was enough of a breakthrough to earn The Strokes a support slot on the GBV's tour for their *Isolation Drills* album. This, along with dozens of other less high profile shows, meant that by the time The Strokes returned to the Mercury Lounge for a residency in late 2000, they were a tight and keenly focussed young band. This was reflected by the increasingly excitable buzz surrounding them.

At the first residency night, the band played to just 50 people. Soon, they had broken the elusive barrier of 100 paying punters and shortly after they were sold-out. At this stage, their fierce dedication was probably their strongest single asset: "We all dropped out of school, quit our jobs, pretty much sacrificed our social lives for a long time, cooping ourselves up in a rehearsal studio from eight at night till eight in the morning. We ate, slept, walked and talked music. We love it. That's the way it should be." This passionate obsession

GUIDED BY VOICES SINGER
BOB POLLARD

was reflected in their rapidly improving live shows, a progression not lost on the local and national American music press, with healthy reviews in *Time Out New York*, *The Village Voice* and two small features in *Rolling Stone*. Although it would be the UK that took to The Strokes first and foremost, those critics with their ears to the ground in the USA knew that here was something they could not afford to ignore.

"The Strokes are Manhattan's first big rock'n'roll thrill of the year," announced the noted music writer David Fricke. "I've seen 'em live, too and they definitely have an album of this stuff in them."

"WE WERE PLAYING SO FUCKING LOUD, HE HEARD US ALL THE WAY ACROSS THE OCEAN!"

RYAN Gentles was carefully selective in choosing who he would receive The Strokes' demo. One copy found its way across the Atlantic to Geoff Travis, music industry maestro and owner of the classic independent record label Rough Trade. Alongside other seminal independents such as Mute and Factory, Rough Trade is one of the UK's most influential and innovative labels. Travis, the son of a Jewish insurance broker, was raised on a mixed diet of Dylan, The Grateful Dead and even a smattering of soul. An English graduate from Churchill College, Cambridge, he gave up a promising teaching career to travel the US, adding to his already prodigiously large record collection at every independent US music store he found along the way. The next logical step was for him to open his own record shop, which he duly did in Kensington Park Road.

The birth of punk coincided with Travis' retail venture and set the tone for his fiercely independent label. He complemented his own ability for talent-spotting with the business acumen of band manager Richard Scott, and this dovetailing of skill meant that Rough Trade records quickly gained itself a formidable reputation. Although it was over 90 singles into its life before it enjoyed its first UK chart success with the number 64 hit, Scritti Politti's

'The Sweetest Girl' in 1981, since then Rough Trade has gone from strength to strength, championing The Smiths and Pulp amongst many others.

Thus Geoff Travis was perhaps perfectly placed to judge The Strokes abrasive three-track demo objectively. Legend has it that he only got halfway through the first song before he knew he wanted to sign them, phoning up Gentles on the spot to make an offer. Interviewed by Ted Kessler in *The Observer,* Travis recalled his gleeful initial reaction: "After about 15 seconds, I agreed to release it. What I heard in The Strokes were the songwriting skills of a first-class writer and music that is a distillation of primal rock'n'roll mixed with the sophistication of today's society. The primitive in the sophisticated, to paraphrase Jean Renoir. It also has an unmacho quality that embodies grace and love, and it touches me." Nick had a rather more earthy view: "We were playing so fucking loud, he heard us all the way across the ocean!"

When Gentles relayed Travis' enthusiasm to the band over dinner, their initial response was muted, more by indifference than ignorance, as Fab explained: "Rough Trade was a name we had heard of and maybe we had noticed it written on one of our albums or something, but it wasn't like, 'Oh man! I really want to get signed to Rough Trade.'" Gentles said Travis wanted them to fly them to England. Armed with a healthy cynicism that would be useful in the forthcoming media frenzy around their band, The Strokes refused to get carried away. "I won't believe this until I have my (plane) ticket - making sure this is true and we weren't kidding ourselves," said Nick.

Gentles understood perfectly the significance of Travis being on board and told the band they should be proud of the fact that he even liked their tape. Furthermore, not only did Travis want to release the demo as *The Modern Age* EP, he'd also insisted on the tape being put out exactly as he had first heard it in demo form, with no big bucks re-recordings, no re-mixing, completely unfettered and tamper-free. Gentles and the band were delighted and flew to the UK to meet Travis. Only a few weeks earlier, Julian was working a bar in New York to scrape in a few dollars; a few weeks later, Oasis' Noel Gallagher would be craning his neck to catch a glimpse of the band at their first UK dates.

GEOFF TRAVIS

THE arrival of The Strokes' demo tape needs to be viewed in the context of the music scene at the time in order to better understand why it made such a seismic impact. The predominant genre in the alternative world at the time was a hybrid son of punk, rap and metal called nu-metal. This latest incarnation of heavy rock reached its commercial zenith with Limp Bizkit, the brainchild of former tattoo artist Fred Durst, whose band enjoyed multi-platinum sales, most famously with their number one *Billboard* album, *Chocolate Starfish And The Hot Dog Flavoured Water*. During the turn of the New Millennium, numerous metal influenced bands enjoyed enormous popularity, including Papa Roach, Staind, Puddle Of Mudd (signed To Durst's own record label), Britain's very own A and the gruesomely masked Slipknot from Des Moins, Iowa.

Durst's own success was assisted by a band widely regarded as being at the original conception of this nu-metal scene – Korn. Alongside The Deftones, Korn released a début album in the early Nineties which set a precedent for all others to follow. Yet the origins of nu-metal can be traced back further than that. Metal had been through numerous incarnations since it inception, with Led Zeppelin generally, but not necessarily accurately, pinned as the grandfathers of the genre thanks to their seminal riff jerker 'Whole Lotta Love'. In truth Zep was a sexy, turbo-charged, electric blues group with a disarmingly un-metal lighter side, and it was bands like Black Sabbath and Judas Priest who really fashioned the format. Elements then seeped into punk, American soft metal and classic British acts such as Iron Maiden showed metal's diversity, while the pull of the underground has seen it splinter off into many subgenres including speed, thrash and extreme metal. Early signs of metal's flexibility had come with the New York rappers Run-DMC's 1986 collaboration with Aerosmith on 'Walk This Way'. The Beastie Boys furthered this liaison, while bands such as Primus, Faith No More and Rage Against The Machine fuelled the genre fusions. Grunge openly worshipped elements of early metal a la Black Sabbath before Green Day and The Offspring reinjected punk into the mix.

KORN'S JONATHAN DAVIS

Nu-metal distinguished itself from all these hybrids by its breadth of influence, drawing in rap, hip hop and electronica to complement the guitars. Nu-metal bands often shared the stage with their DJs and the vocals blended rapping, singing and metal rage. Baseball caps were worn back-to-front, pants were short and very baggy, goatee beards were essential and everything had to be played very loud.

LIMP BIZKIT

However, as with every scene which dominates the charts for long, bored detractors soon complained of identikit nu-metal bands. Linkin Park boasted the biggest selling album of 2001 with *Hybrid Theory* but were seen by many observers as contrived. Limp Bizkit, who in 2000 could seemingly do no wrong, were slated for being too corporate, with Fred Durst's record company career being highlighted as symptomatic of the band's 'selling out'. Yet by the tale end of 2000, there were still many nu-metal bands selling a lot of records. Elsewhere, hip hop continued to wallow in often misogynist and self-reverential cliché, while the pop market was sated with puppet-like boy/girl bands and the TV phenomenon that was *Popstars* and further stoked by the commercial behemoth that was *Pop Idol*.

So The Strokes' demo arrived at a time when a clutch of acts were repeatedly selling vast quantities of records. Nonetheless, over the din of commercial success, increasingly dissatisfied voices bemoaned the repetitive machismo of nu-metal, the corniness of mainstream hip hop, the saccharine and transparent sterility of pop and the general malaise of guitar bands such as Elbow, Coldplay and Starsailor. Even the street sounds of So Solid Crew and the emerging garage scene did not stem the sensation that the time was ripe for fresh blood. Enter The Strokes.

Julian was bemused by all the music histrionics. He was not a fan of nu-metal, obviously, saying, "Stuff like Limp Bizkit and Korn – that's not balls to me. That's fake, like putting steroids in your body." Yet, for him, there was no relevance to which scene was fading and which one they represented. "We're not purposely trying to be different than anything else going on. The bottom line is we don't really listen to the radio. We're not really into what's popular. We've been sort of doing our own thing. So I think our product is pretty modern, but it's definitely not modern in terms of what's popular today."

THIS was the world into which The Strokes released their first record, *The Modern Age EP*, on Rough Trade in March, 2001. Despite little press coverage to speak of, the EP sold an impressive 3,000 copies. More notable than their modest yet encouraging sales, however, was the reaction of the British music press to their arrival, in particular *NME*.

It was at the very start of 2001 that The Strokes feted demo tape first landed on the desks at *NME*. Instantly recognising their potential, that paper embarked on a love affair with the New Yorkers as passionate as any they'd conducted with favoured acts before. The role of the *NME*, and to a lesser extent *The Face*, in the enormous media, music industry and subsequent public interest in The Strokes cannot be underestimated.

To understand the importance of this we need to take a look at the state of the UK music press at the time The Strokes emerged. After 75 years the venerable weekly *Melody Maker,* once referred to as The Bible, published its final issue with the 2001 Christmas edition, leaving *NME* as the only UK weekly alternative music magazine in a market that had once supported a shelf-full of titles. The metal-heads magazine *Kerrang!* was also enjoying a spectacular spell of popularity, thanks in part to the success of the nu-metal bands, but also due to perceptive editing and a positive, laddish-like, approach to reviewing bands. Thus it was with some fanfare that in early 2002 *Kerrang!* announced that for the first time their circulation had surpassed that of *NME*, an achievement unthinkable during the latter's heyday of 200,000-plus copies a week. The irony was that *NME* now had the field to itself, its fiercest rivals, in the shape of *Melody Maker, Sounds, Vox* and *Select*, all now having bitten the dust.

In tandem with its falling circulation, *NME* had been the subject of repeated criticism for promoting a so-called 'build-them-up, knock-them-down'

culture in the music press. Weekly publications demand fresh news – and fresh faces - on a much quicker basis than monthly magazines and, perhaps out of a necessity caused by the dearth of superstar names, *NME* and, in its death throes, *Melody Maker* found themselves constantly scouring the UK to find new acts to grace their front covers. Indeed, it seemed at times as if their journalists were becoming A&R men themselves, discovering acts before even the record labels could sign them up. The downside of this, of course, was that their readers were subjected to articles about acts they'd never heard of, a state of affairs that flew in the face of the accepted rule that big names on the cover sold magazines. A prime example of this in the Nineties was when the *Maker* plastered Suede on their front page above the banner headline, 'The Best New Band In Britain'. Fortunately for Brett Andersen et al, his act was accomplished enough to withstand the sudden media spotlight and industry expectation that this PR coup brought.

"HERE IS A BAND THAT HAD EVERYTHING - THE LOOK, THE SOUND, THE ATTITUDE, THE WHOLE THING"

Others were not so fortunate. Menswear were similarly lauded, as were Gay Dad, but both stumbled and fell. In this regard overly favourable *NME* coverage was becoming something of a poisoned chalice. Few aspiring young groups would turn down the opportunity of a flattering *NME* lead feature, but it took a level-headedness beyond the capacity of most to negotiate the ensuing media frenzy without imploding in terminal and abject failure.

The Strokes were hailed as the latest in a long line of bands who were going to "save rock". Previous recent messiahs bearing this weighty burden included Starsailor, ...And You Will Know Us By The Trail Of Dead, Queens Of The Stone Age and Texan quintet At The Drive In. This last band made no secret of their discomfort with such media glare, preferring to inhabit a comfortable underground where they had already been gigging for eight years. All this, of course, assumes that you agree rock needs saving...

NME ignored such criticisms and nailed their colours firmly to the mast very early on with The Strokes. Take this tribute from an article in late spring 2001: "The clipped, pulsating swagger of their first single marked (The Strokes) out as the best debut for about a million years, and... the last time they were in England, their gigs were a revelation [more of which later]. Here is a band that had everything - the look, the sound, the attitude, the whole thing." *NME* 'Single Of The Week' was a given, hailing the EP's "clattering subway groove, a perfect collision between The Velvet Underground's 'Run Run Run' and The Jam's 'David Watts'. It wasn't just *NME*, the music press in general had finally found the band they'd looking for since the demise of Britpop - hence long before The Strokes even released their début album they had already been captured for cover features on both *NME* and *Time Out.*

The Strokes did not expect to receive such unreserved media plaudits, nor could they have envisaged that the *NME*'s enthusiasm be matched by almost every other music publication in the UK. Within one year of surfacing, The Strokes had received more column inches than most bands command in an entire career.

To their credit, The Strokes seemed more than aware of the possible downside of such a positive media profile. Fab reflected on their coverage and said, "I appreciate that but... I hope our music is good enough to sustain that, you know what I mean? When the *NME*, for example, says that we're 'the best band to come about in 25 years', I surely do not agree with that... I think the repercussion to all of this hype is going to be pretty heavy, but the fact that we're not interested in the hype to begin with, we're probably not going to be interested in how it backlashes."

Jealous bands and industry cynics became The Strokes' fiercest enemies, and some criticism seemed justified, even if it wasn't The Strokes themselves who were strictly to blame. One angry letter writer to the *NME* was forced to express his disdain when that paper reported that The Strokes had composed a new song: "Look here, I know how desperate you are for any kind of news concerning The Strokes but this is fucking ludicrous. 'The Strokes write song!' So fucking what? They're musicians. That's what they do! Jeezus, it's like 'Postman delivers letter!' or 'Bus Driver Drives Bus!'"

CHAPTER SIX

"WHAT A SMALL THING TO TALK ABOUT, THE HOURS YOU SPEND ON MUSIC COMPARED TO THE MINUTES YOU SPEND ON WHAT YOU'RE GOING TO WEAR"

ALBERT HAMMOND

THE very first live taste of The Strokes in the UK occurred at an *NME*/Carling show in January, 2001 supporting ...And You Will Know Us By The Trail Of Dead, at the humble Wedgewood Rooms in Portsmouth. This modest start was followed by four more dates, including one at the Astoria and the Camden Monarch in central London (the latter on the same night that a resurgent U2 played the capital). The Monarch show in particular saw an attendance of A&R and media 'names' on a scale rarely seen.

Leaving the salivating press and public behind, The Strokes headed back to their native USA, where their profile was altogether rather different, ie virtually negligible. Here, The Strokes were faced with the soul-destroying obligation to play a month long series of dates and semi-residencies at Boston and Philadelphia venues, including a residency at the 250-capacity Khyber Pass bar. To make matters worse, self-imposed financial prudence demanded avoiding hotels, thus necessitating a four-hour round trip from New York each night. By day the band would rehearse at their usual Hell's Kitchen studio, then as night drew in they would hump their gear into the back of their dishevelled van and start the long journey to The Khyber for their midnight show. A duo of shows here was complemented by two gigs at the oddly named TT The Bear's in Boston and three more in Philadelphia at The 5 Spot and then Transit.

While Noel Gallagher was telling all who would listen in the UK that The Strokes were the future of rock'n'roll, in the urban wasteland of Philadelphia, the band were afforded no such celebrity favours. In stark contrast to Rough Trade's plans for feverish record store signings in England in the summer,

The Strokes found themselves selling their own CDs after the gig at their New England and Philly shows in May 2001. Nick had to scrawl posters himself and set up a stall selling the CDs for $5 each. They were shifting about a dozen or so each night. At one show, their sound engineer for the gig was actually in one of the other two bands also playing that evening and was repeatedly distracted by drunken celebrations for his own stag night.

A strange dichotomy was rife. While Julian was comparing his band to other US acts who still had day jobs, across the pond in Britain a legion of journalists and fellow rock stars were hailing them as the great white hope. With Geoff Travis having endorsed the band so heavily and their début EP doing such solid initial business, it was only a matter of time before record companies back in the USA started to take an interest. The low profile shows

"ACTUALLY, WE HAVEN'T EVEN MET ANYONE WEARING A SUIT. ALBERT'S DRESSED BETTER THAN ANY EXECUTIVES WE'VE MET"

at the Khyber and other nearby venues had seduced many nervous A&R into a trip to Philadelphia or Boston, eager not to miss out on this next-big-thing. With the dawning realisation that much of the US record business was already onto The Strokes, the corporate cheque books started opening with alarming rapidity.

Suddenly, instead of counting small change and adding up a meagre wafer of greenbacks, The Strokes were in meetings with major record labels falling over themselves in a bid to secure their five signatures. A barn-storming set at CMJ Music Marathon in New York followed by a rabble-rousing show at Austin's South by Southwest music conference had all ratcheted up the intense interest. Less than twelve months previous, their average gig attendance was under fifty; now their days were spent discussing which seven figure record deal might be the one for them.

Julian even took a 4am phone call from the Head of RCA America who raved about the brilliance of their music. His efforts were rewarded when, after much industry battling, RCA managed to sign The Strokes, reportedly for an advance in excess on $1 million. They had barely toured their home country, unusual for a territory that demands extensive dues are paid (and many a band broken) before contracts are exchanged.

RCA agreed to concede full artistic control to the band, unusual for a début record deal, and it is rumoured they were the only label not to walk away when the band suggested they would never make a video. "The whole thing about videos is that sometimes it takes away from good songs and then it makes boring songs entertaining to look at," protested Julian. The record company did, however, scupper rumours of seven figure advances, as their Senior Vice President of A&R, Steve Ralbovsky, told *Blender* magazine:

"The up-front dollars were nowhere near that. The Strokes weren't piggish or greedy. I've seen bands with less attention get a great deal more, but the road is littered with their bodies. The Strokes know that." He also voiced an admirable degree of restraint over their career development, saying, "Our challenge is to be patient. People are so ready for a fountainhead band to lead the way out of rock music's malaise, but you've got to be careful about those expectations." The band could sense this corporate poise: "RCA was the closest we could get to a major label understanding a small rock group," Nik recalled. "We were pretty confident that it would work. At the same time, we listened to them if they had suggestions. For us, it was an ideal situation. We were aiming more for creative control. We liked what we did and we just wanted to continue that.

Sort of like an independent way to look at it with major label backing."

RCA were the lucky ones, The Strokes seemed to like them. Legend has it that at one gig, a still-unsigned Strokes were playing to a crowd of several hundred, which included many music business executives. Julian spotted one particular 'talent scout' looking at his watch in almost total indifference. After observing several more dismissive glances at his wrist, Julian exploded mid-song, screaming "Don't you fucking look at your watch while I'm singing!" before returning to the melody, without missing a note.

RCA were not embarrassed that it had taken a UK independent to pick up on the phenomenon that was sitting right under their noses, as Steve Ralbovsky explained: "I'm not surprised that they happened in England first. There's a long tradition of primitive American rock'n'roll being absorbed there first, and the Strokes have that elemental quality."

Inevitably, The Strokes signing to RCA solicited numerous calls of 'selling out', a tiresome whine often heard when any new band decides to work 'for the man'. Wisely, The Strokes were utterly dismissive of such indie fascism, citing various reasons for their ease at being on a major label. Nick saw it as an easy choice: "They just give us money and stay out of our way," while Albert was somewhat more flippant, saying "It's like being bisexual. Yeah, you get the best of both worlds." As for selling out to the men in suits, Julian says, "Actually, we haven't even met anyone wearing a suit. Albert's dressed better than any executives we've met."

AT the time of The Strokes' UK success, much was being made of the almost total failure of British acts to puncture the US charts. Indeed the polarity between the two countries as far as popular music goes, seems to be greater now that at any time since the emergence of The Beatles in the early Sixties. In April, 2002, no singles by British acts were registered in the *Billboard* Top 100 for the first time in 38 years. Only two were found on the album charts, specifically Craig David's *Born To Do It* and Ozzy Osbourne's *Down To Earth*, the latter no doubt fuelled by Osbourne's decidedly American profile (and home), as seen in the MTV smash hit reality show, *The Osbournes*. The Strokes' more modest popularity in the USA was oddly inconsistent with this homegrown bias in their charts.

Since the Fifties teenager first started buying records, transatlantic cultural sparring between US and UK music has inspired healthy competition. Elvis exploded in the UK in 1956 but six years later The Beatles hit back with 'I Want To Hold Your Hand', which opened the floodgates of Beatlemania in the States, just as 'She Loves You' had done in the UK. The Mop Tops' chart-topping single launched a period of unprecedented UK dominance in the US charts. The cultural and commercial impact was so great that Prime Minister Douglas-Home called the besuited foursome 'my secret weapon', and some observers were even moved to remark that Britain had not exerted this much influence on the USA since the American Revolution of 1775. The subsequent British invasion of the American charts was so complete that the federal government began denying visas to UK acts to stem the flood of British music stars outselling their US rivals. After The Beatles had broken down the barriers, others gleefully followed suit. Due to its global impact and subsequent cultural legacy, 'I Want To Hold Your Hand' has been described as 'possibly the most important song in the history of rock'.

British exports to the States continued unabated until the mid-Eighties. As pop became rock and stages sagged beneath the weight of massive speakers, The Rolling Stones, The Who and Led Zeppelin led a charge that reaped a massive harvest of greenbacks from row upon row of rabid fans in huge arenas designed for pro-sport. Even after the punk watershed occasional one-ff successes like Wham!, Depeche Mode and later Bush held the fort for British exports to the States, though as the Nineties progressed the fort was looking less and less secure. Grunge's omnipresent loser culture provided the catalyst for the irony-drenched melodies of Britpop; three years after Cobain's death The Prodigy became only the seventh British act to enter the America album charts at number one with *The Fat Of The Land* in 1997. America retaliated with nu-metal and for a while Britain had no answer. Then came The Strokes. They were neither a reaction to a British musical phenomenon, nor were they born out of a hatred for groups in red baseball caps and baggy pants. They were just The Strokes.

THE Strokes have won acres of media coverage based on the clothes they wear. Fashion bible *The Face* helped greatly in this, publishing a substantial feature on them at a seemingly super-early phase in their career. The Strokes have even surfaced in women's glossy, *Elle*. Of course, such superficial emphasis inevitably fuelled accusations that they more style than substance, insults the individual members of the band find most offensive. The misunderstanding that "we're in this for anything other than the music, that were fashionistas, that we're rich boys trying to steal the spotlight from someone else" troubles Fab deeply.

It is a little odd that The Strokes have caused such a ruckus in the fashion world. What they wear is hardly revolutionary, clearly derivative and easily traceable. Yet, so much fashion burns brightly in this endless cycle of reincarnation that The Strokes have both a surprising look and, by contrast,

"I GET FUNNY LOOKS IF I'M IN A WEIRD NEIGHBOURHOOD, BUT SO WHAT?"

one that is actually quite predictable. They are all fashionably skinny (though none have ever been to a gym), often looking like they are at the wrong end of a very long night. They wear faded denim jackets (*a la* Shakin' Stevens, hardly a man to trouble fashion experts). There are the casual sports tops from another era, straight out of your uncle's wardrobe; the black leather jackets, an essential item from just about any classic rock era; and the occasional pair of Dr Martens boots and band T-shirts, including The White Stripes and Nirvana. Then there's the pinstripe suit jackets with Converse trainers, and faded shirts with trousers just a little too short on length, sometimes mixed with (your Grandad's favourite) cords. The stylishly dishevelled effect is often capped with a thin tie, recalling Blondie at their peak. Some of the band's jackets are expensive designer labels; one of Nikolai's cost $1 from a Salvation Army shop.

Then there are the hair cuts. Possibly cut by themselves, possibly trimmed for $200 in an arty salon by a man with an extravagantly manicured beard. Some of their barnets are limp and straggled, others shorter, more tousled. Albert has the best cut, a bird's nest of curls perched on top of his cartoonish face. Julian has been known to prepare for a glossy photo shoot by ruffling his hair into place with beer. The final detail is the Marlboro cigarette hanging indifferently from the corner of a mouth – clichéd when drooping out of a soft rockers lips but, somehow, not here. The US version of 'Hard To Explain' was sent to the printers of Marlboro packets, so the band could ensure an exact match for their red and white sleeve.

And what about Julian: for many, the perfect frontman. He conjures up images of Iggy, Jagger, Lou Reed, Anthony Kiedis, even Liam Gallagher, all rolled into one, a rock icon for the new Millennium. The 'look' is not manufactured nor is it entirely accidental. Julian used to put on stage gear for each show, but Nick scorned this approach, telling him instead to "dress every day like you're going to play a show". This fashion tenet has since become an unofficial band motto. "I get funny looks if I'm in a weird neighbourhood, but so what?" Albert is universally credited with shaping much of The Strokes' look – ever the stylist, he once proposed to a girl with a ring made from a twisted and folded dollar bill… she said "maybe".

This is hardly high fashion, but somehow The Strokes seem to pull it off. They ought to look as if someone is playing Fantasy Rock Stars and has plucked all the best bits from CBGBs, US garage punk, from Lou Reed, Joey Ramone and an encyclopaedia of rock history. Except they don't. Perhaps, as with their music, The Strokes' X-factor is their ability to create something that is very much more than the sum of their obvious parts.

The Strokes also possess that rare quality which Oasis so obviously boasted, which The Stone Roses had for a brief while and which Kurt Cobain seemed to have every time a photographer's lens clicked: the ability to generate immediate iconographic photography, instant rock archive. Their photographs and album mug shots appear both timeless and time-specific, a historical snapshot that is but a few seconds old. Each fashion magazine shoot seems to add to their image, each record sleeve reinforcing that status. They look like they are a band from the pages of a book on classic rock photography, wizened by years on the road and defiantly ramshackle in their rock'n'roll appearance. Yet, they have only played less than a couple of hundred gigs.

CHAPTER SEVEN

"YOU'RE NOT THE FIRST TO THINK THAT EVERYTHING HAS BEEN THOUGHT BEFORE"

PAUL DEMPSEY FROM SOMETHING FOR KATE

SEIZING upon the extraordinary response in the UK, Geoff Travis and the band agreed on a 16–date UK tour which, remarkably for such a new act but not so remarkably in view of the media scrum, was a sell-out. *NME* were obviously there to review these shows and offered this no holds barred tribute: "Let's be blunt and say The Strokes are the coolest motherfuckers around right now. They swoon with the pure romance and passion of Punk Rock NYC, swaggering street-poets who thrash out towering pop songs awash with love and hate and lust and the switchblade-agony of misunderstanding, all the frustrations of young adulthood writ in Technicolor widescreen with casual profundity by photogenic Bowery bards." Another gig was reviewed thus: "They look and sound like the band who are going to save rock... The Strokes really are perfect. Without doubt the greatest band to emerge from New York for two decades. That they're intent on getting better is a frightening prospect. A band like The Strokes only comes along once in a lifetime. You should be grateful that they've come along in yours."

By now, their UK profile was almost unmatched and was certainly unique at the time for a band yet to release an album. Noel Gallagher again made it known he wanted them to support the mighty Oasis, a compliment he had paid to many bands previously, including perhaps most famously Travis. At the Oxford Zodiac show on June 12, supermodel Kate Moss was in attendance along with designer-to-the-stars Stella McCartney, Paul's seamstress daughter. So was the diminutive Radiohead frontman, Thom Yorke. So many music journalists wanted to see the show that a mini bus was hired to ferry them en masse up the M40 motorway. Also on this tour, Joe Strummer of The Clash was spotted at the back of the crowd beaming throughout and he later told a bemused and delighted Strokes that it was the first time in years he could remember smiling all the way through a gig. Elton John was a virtual lone beacon of indifference, saying the band were too referential and retrogressive.

Aside from the celebratory fans, the tour was hardly uneventful. In Glasgow for the show at King Tut's Wah Wah Hut on June 20, Fabrizio broke his wrist when he fell out off the tour bus (he was sober!). Some shows were inevitably cancelled, including a sprinkling of these UK gigs and some Australian dates. Fab actually travelled down under hoping to recuperate in time but was forced to give in to doctor's orders and hand his drum sticks over.

"THEY LOOK AND SOUND LIKE THE BAND WHO ARE GOING TO SAVE ROCK... THE STROKES REALLY ARE PERFECT"

With another seven UK shows plus an extensive European début tour already lined up, the band flew in old friend and drummer Matt Romano, formerly of the Selzers, as a temporary replacement. Even then there were problems, as Romano's passport was out of date and his new one only arrived in time for him to squeeze in last minute rehearsals before the band's tour continued. Six dates throughout Europe and a bristling performance at Glasgow's T In The Park festival brilliantly served to crank up the fervour around The Strokes one more notch. By now, touts in major cities were asking for – and getting – upwards of £180 a ticket. At this point, The Strokes' youthful enthusiasm carried them through this slew of dates, as reflected by this endearingly innocent quote from Julian: "I find touring very similar to vacation. You get to go in a van, hang out with friends, go to towns you've never been to before. And on top of it, you get to play a show!"

These dates were centred around the release of The Strokes' second UK single, the double A-side 'Hard To Explain'/'New York Cops'. This was a perfect riposte to the swelling band of cynics, who seemed to multiply in direct proportion to the band's growing press profile. The release was an abrasive blast, a reinforcement of their intentions to re-introduce rock'n'roll to the masses, the perfect antidote to nu-metal overdose. Critics were quick to point towards the double A-side as dripping with 1976 New York flavour, although there are also snatches of the UK's Wire and, more recently and perhaps more obviously, a slice of Dave Gedge's The Wedding Present. The release was a powerful combination and was, in retrospect, destined to become the band's first UK Top 20 success, charting as it did at number 16. This earned them their début appearance on *Top Of The Pops*, which they universally agreed was a fantastic experience.

By the sixteenth and final UK show at London's 1,200 capacity Heaven on June 28, press coverage and celebrity hype around the band was reaching epidemic proportions. Unexpected media adoration was supplemented by a carefully planned and saturated campaign of advertising by their supportive record company. This show was touted heavily and at the after-show party, the band could hardly move for industry admirers wanting to chat to them (rumours suggest that this time even Stella McCartney could not gain entry). Despite their popularity, or more likely because of it, snipers at the back of the venue were already whispering about a backlash. Natural cynicism aside, The Strokes' were acutely aware that their meteoric rise to fame demanded appropriately top quality material. In the world of the single, The Strokes had already proved they were more than up to the fight; the question was, could that momentum and quality be sustained over the course of their début album, which would inevitably be the most hyped – and most keenly analysed – long player of the year.

THE Strokes sound like The Velvet Underground. They look a bit like Velvet Underground. Some say they are merely an excuse for music writers to write yet more about Velvet Underground. Well, here goes. To a generation of kids brought up on Fred Durst and P Diddy, whose idea of an old rock song is an early Nirvana track, the reference points thrown around The Strokes' lineage might seem a little obtuse. The obvious and most aired comparison is with Velvet Underground.

VELVET UNDERGROUND - MAUREEN TUCKER, LOU REED, JOHN CALE AND STERLING MORRISON

Velvet Underground became a cult band in the mid-to-late Sixties. Spearheaded by guitarist and songwriter Lou Reed and the classically trained multi-instrumentalist John Cale, they were anathema to much of what was happening in the musical and cultural world at the time. Like The Strokes, they were New Yorkers at heart. Cale studied in New York, on a Leonard Bernstein scholarship; Reed studied at Syracuse University, which is where he met VU guitarist Sterling Morrison. Unlike The Strokes, however, putative leader Reed had paid his dues before he joined the band and had even spent time as a contracted songwriter for Pickwick Records. In keeping with their slightly sleazy image, the band's name was inspired by the tile of a risqué paperback book whose jacket featured thigh-high boots, a mask and a whip, and they recruited Nico, a sultry German model, to sing.

Their avante garde 1967 début album *Velvet Underground And Nico*, though largely unheralded at the time and a commercial disaster, established them as an outfit capable of strikingly unorthodox songwriting with an emphasis on minimalism and despair. The sparse production and air of doom separated them from the prevailing musical mood of hippiedom and psychedelia. They were closely associated with pop art guru Andy Warhol, who became something of a band mentor. Indeed, it's quite possible that Warhol saw them as an artistic statement in themselves, a sort of performance art exhibit to stand alongside the silk-screen paintings and art films that his Factory workshop was producing.

After Warhol's arrival as manager, Velvet Underground themselves played a New York residency, this time at the Café Bizarre, but the rest of America was largely oblivious to their charms. The début album, with its songs about drugs and low life, reached no higher than number 171 on the US charts on its initial release. One observer later said, "Hardly anybody bought it, but everyone who did formed a band." Nico quit before the follow-up, their classic *White Light, White Heat*, reportedly recorded in just one day at the end of a lengthy tour, was another commercial flop. Then Cale quit after a row with Reed. Two further albums followed before the band fragmented and the individuals embarked on solo careers with varying degrees of success, most notably perhaps when Lou Reed worked with Bowie and Mick Ronson on the seminal *Transformer* album. Reunion projects in the early Nineties met with strong critical acclaim, though tensions between the autocratic Reed and the others, notably Cale, scuppered any hopes of a lasting relationship. Morrison died in 1995. In years following the Velvets' initial demise, they come to be regarded as one of the most innovative and influential acts of all-time.

There are several obvious parallels with Velvet Underground worth highlighting, the most pertinent of which is the similarity in vocal delivery between Lou Reed and Julian Casablancas. Reed sang about unusually harsh topics with the VU – sado-masochism, paranoia and heroin – but it is the delivery of those lines that seems to embody a direct antecedence to Julian. Reed sang with an urgent distraction, giving the impression of being uninterested in what he was singing about, yet at the same time he was deeply and intimately committed to each and every word. It created a certain emotional distance and aloofness that few bands can master, though Blondie's Debbie Harry was able to communicate a similar sense of detachment, seemingly bored with, yet in love with, their own songs at the same time.

Julian sings in a manner akin to much of the early Velvet Underground material. Rifling through albums such as *White Light, White Heat* can offer various examples of this similarity in tracks such as 'I'm Waiting For The Man' and, later, the more melodic 'Sweet Jane'. Julian has admitted that when he wrote 'The Modern Age' he was listening to a lot of Velvet Underground, having bought his first record by them aged just 14. Of course, the New York accent helps. It is hard to imagine The Strokes would have garnered quite the same 'cool' factor and gritty ambience had their vocalist hailed from Basingstoke, even if he did use overdrive and distortion on his voice.

Julian explained how… "I think the biggest thing that I took personally from Velvet Underground is trying to do something so raw but at the same time I really like beautiful, powerful melody." Velvet Underground is the one band that the whole of The Strokes can unanimously agree upon liking.

"I MEAN, FUCK IT. WHY NOT SOUND LIKE THAT? IT SOUNDS BETTER THAN ANY OF THE SHIT AROUND TODAY"

The Strokes' guitars also evoke the Velvets. The latter used simple, on the beat guitar work, no wild self-indulgent solos and a very clipped delivery. This gave their music – and likewise The Strokes – a sense of urgency and musical anxiety that filled each song with energy. Tracing the lineage back still further, Buddy Holly was perhaps the master of this technique, hitting most of his chords on the downstroke only, offering no soothing counterpoint on the up stroke that might have softened the pace. The Velvets and The Strokes both quote from Holly in that sense, though Holly's songs derive from a far more innocent age. The Strokes' brief, smart guitar riffs all smack of classic Velvet Underground and the rhythm guitars seem to follow in a direct family line.

Valensi is a huge fan of Velvets' guitarist Sterling Morrison, so perhaps the similarities are inevitable (Albert points out that their guitars are also close to The Ramones, a band they are happy to cite as a key influence). The Strokes use more complex drums but the essence of their purpose – and production – is much the same.

Of course, certain elements of The Strokes are nothing like Velvet Underground – The Strokes' recorded brevity is a shared passion, but there is (as yet) no 'Sister Ray', the 17-minute epic from the Velvets' second album.

These occasional lapses into prolonged musical indulgence separate these two bands – for now.

Visually there are clear comparisons. Velvet Underground wore black leather jackets and faded jeans with shades, at a time when most rock stars and their fans were in crushed velvet flares and wildly colourful kaftan coats. The Velvets, like The Beatles before them, put cool clothes back into music. Like The Strokes, they were perennially sullen and both acts seem to epitomise in band form the dirty, noisey swagger of New York.

Furthermore, it is not just on Velvets' records that their influence can be picked up. No doubt The Strokes will have also listened to David Bowie tracks such as 'Queen Bitch' on the album *Hunky Dory*, which was a direct nod to Velvet Underground – Bowie himself used to play 'White Light/White Heat' and 'I'm Waiting For The Man' live.

The Strokes didn't just feel inspired by the Velvets' actual songs – the production was key too. They relish the simplicity of the Velvets' production and the direct approach of The Ramones. "You don't need 72 mikes on a drum kit to record a song - just put one on the bass drum, one up there and one in the corner somewhere and you're fine, you'll get a much cooler sound," says Fab.

Where The Strokes share no mutual ground with the Velvets is in their media impact. At the time of their emergence, the Velvets were strictly underground, cherished only by a select band of knowledgeable fans. Only later did their true importance and enormous influence become clear, as music historians correctly highlighted them as one of the key bands in the 20th century. Yet The Strokes, careering along the ultra-fast super highway of the new media age, are in a very different situation. While the Velvets' début was largely ignored, both by the public and an unsupportive label, The Strokes' first album has shoved them into the glare of expectation and their influence – if any – is already being prematurely judged.

MOST great bands suffer from accusations of plagiarism: Elvis cannibalised black music for commercial gain; Dylan was faking Woodie Guthrie and far too referential with his eponymous début album; The Rolling Stones tipped of countless black blues performers; Nirvana merely Americanised Black Sabbath, and so on. Music cannot move forward without first looking back.

Fab made no secret of The Strokes' retro record collection: "I mean, fuck it. Why not sound like that? It sounds better than any of the shit around today. Sure, we have looked back, but it wasn't because we wanted to steal anything or be like anyone. We were just music fans looking for good music; and that was where we found it." To this day they still rifle through the shelves of numerous back street second-hand record stores in New York, such as their favourite Final Vinyl on 6th Street.

However, as the band repeatedly point out themselves, Velvet Underground are just one of a myriad of influences on their music and look. The nods towards Television, The Ramones and Blondie are all relevant, although Valensi said of the former that… "I'd never heard Television until people said we sounded like them and when I heard them I didn't like them. They've got no balls in their playing."

The reason The Strokes are mentioned in the same breath as the New York downtown scene of the Seventies – Television, The Ramones, Talking Heads even – is because those bands were heavily influenced by Velvet Underground themselves. They merely share the same genetics. Julian was not afraid to shy away from pointing this out: "I think Velvet Underground blow all those late Seventies bands away. That's my opinion. No offence to anyone who likes those bands. That's cool. But people keep telling us we sound like that and I'm not going for that."

The Strokes' sound is pure New York, but one that draws most of all on the Velvets – the hints of dingy gigs in CBGBs is indeed merely a by-product. If anything, The Strokes are perhaps most influenced by NEW YORK, rather than any one New York band. Fab admits: "When you come from the city, there's a certain vibe that comes across in your music. It's not necessarily in the notes that you play and the lyrics that you sing; it's just a little bit of the energy. You've got a bunch of people stacked all on top of each other here, so there's gonna be that little taste of New York in the music."

Admirers said the city hadn't produced such a band since Sonic Youth or maybe The Beastie Boys (positive comparisons would later be made with Sonic Youth's *NYC Ghosts & Flowers* album). Others asked how it was possible to be a modern garage band in a city where a car park space costs $1,500 a month.

When a band come along who are as venerated as The Strokes, it is inevitable that a whole melting pot of references are thrown in – it makes them seem more cool and therefore, by association, their fans. So we have it that they sound like The Stooges, Blondie, The Ramones, Television, New York Dolls, Elvis Costello, The Smiths…. Interestingly, despite regular protestations to look beyond such archivist reference points, The Strokes are not averse to dropping in obscure musical reference points themselves, such as the occasional live tribute to the technically meticulous thrash band Anacrusis.

BEFORE we leave the Velvets it's worth mentioning that Nick once bumped into Lou Reed, whose famously aloof nature was on display at the time. He retold the story, his words still brimming with excitement, to *Juice* magazine: "Recently at the movies, Lou Reed was there in the line and I was really freaked out that I was right next to him - Lou Reed! It was really crowded (when I got) in the movie theatre. We just went right down the front and after about five minutes, I turned my head and there's Lou Reed sitting in the seat next to me. I don't think I paid a second's attention to what happened on the screen. We were going to see *Blow*, that Johnny Depp film, and I don't remember any of it. All I remember thinking for an hour and a half was: 'Man, that's Lou Reed.' …

"I couldn't help myself, I just had to go, 'Hey, I'm just a huge fan, and I know you get this all the time,' and he didn't look amused at all. Just out of curiosity I said, 'Have you ever heard of a band called The Strokes?' and he just looked at me and said, 'No', really grumpy and short."

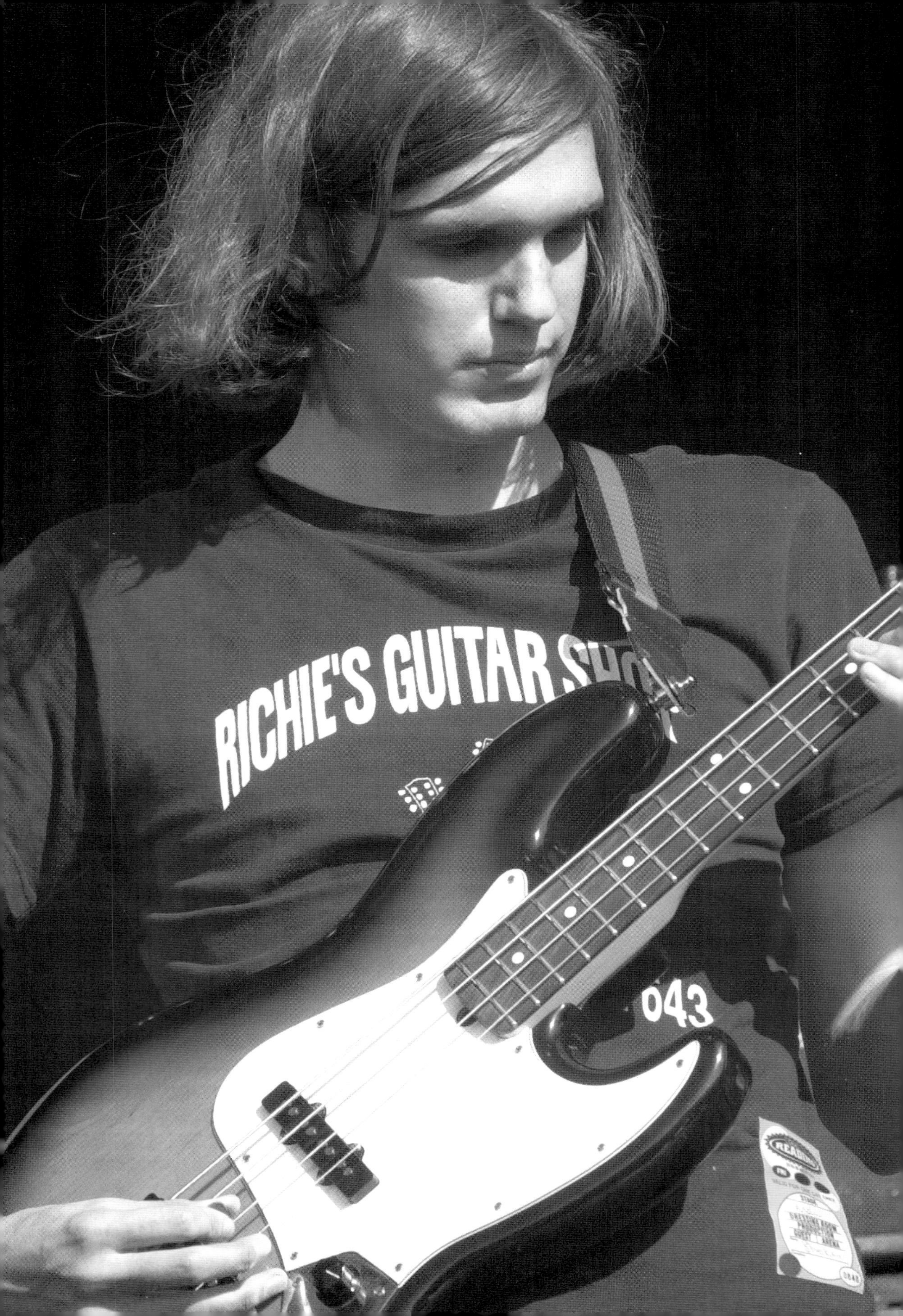
RICHIE'S GUITAR
043

CHAPTER EIGHT

"ON STAGE I MAKE LOVE TO 25,000 PEOPLE. THEN I GO HOME ALONE"

JANIS JOPLIN

AFTER the Australian and European tours had ended, The Strokes headed back home for six shows in North America, including the famous Troubadour in LA, and a feverishly received pair of gigs at the Summer Sonic Festival in Osaka and Tokyo. Next up was their biggest show to date, the UK's Reading Festival 2001. Originally billed for one of the numerous smaller stages, the band was subsequently 'promoted' to the main stage, thanks largely to their exaggerated press profile, and in particular a concerted campaign by *NME* to move them higher up the bill and into the main arena. Just seven months previously they had played their début UK show as a support band in Portsmouth's tiny Wedgewood Rooms.

This annual August Bank Holiday weekend festival had recently spread its wings to include a sister event in Leeds with each day's bill rotated at each venue. Traditionally, Reading is renowned for lesser known bands making their breakthrough, often on one of the smaller stages – but already The Strokes found themselves sharing the main stage with Travis, Iggy Pop and Green Day. Julian admitted to being starstruck when he met Iggy and Green Day and was later wracked by his severest stage nerves yet, vomiting copiously before going out to perform. He needn't have worried: sandwiched between Eels and Iggy, The Strokes were fanatically received.

Backstage at Reading was rife with rumours suggesting Courtney Love had written a song about Julian, entitled 'But Julian, I'm A Little Older Than You'. This in turn led to more rumours about Julian fancying the Hole frontwoman.

He admitted he had met her but played down any romance, pointing out how helpful she had been: "That was kind of weird for me, but she was pretty normal, I guess... I think it's because we had this talk. She was just giving me advice, I think."

This festival show was a fine example of his band's excellent live set too. They have the archetypal rock band presence on stage. Bassist Fraiture is painfully shy, nailed to the stage in the time-honoured tradition of immobile bass players best personified by the late great John Entwistle. He is happy to let the rest of The Strokes thrash around, with the usual 'animal' on drums in the shape of Fab Moretti. Nick and Albert take it in turns to absorb the spotlight while Julian parades around the boards like a cock-sure young rock singer should do. Occasionally (although not at Reading!) he will plunge into the crowd while Fab has been known to execute an extremely high quality stagedive. This is not a headbanging, arms thrashing *Kerrang!* spectacle, but with a set list like theirs, The Strokes do not need to try too hard.

The Strokes have earned a reputation for partying on the road. Their tour bus is always resonating with deafening music, often by Bob Marley or even A-Ha. In amongst the newspapers and pornographic videos lie dog-eared copies of numerous classic novels by writers such as Bukowski, James Joyce, Kurt Vonnegut and Jung. However, don't think The Strokes enjoy late night bus reading groups with a glass of wine and a slice of cheese. With such feted looks and celebrated style, they find themselves constantly besieged by groupies and hangers-on. However, for a band as young both in years and career, they appear to have an acute and surprising awareness of the pitfalls of over-indulgence. Being deliberately evasive, they will say only that the rigours of touring have, on a few occasions, forced their notoriously close friendships to breaking point. Certain members of the band have had to be persuaded from "partying too hard" and Nikolai for one feels that a split was not an impossibility on more than one occasion: "Looking back on it we know that it's pressure from touring... mistakes like partying too much and not concentrating on why you're actually here which is the music and us as friends." Even if they did split, Fab says he will walk away having had "the most spectacular time in my life..."

and as long as they remained friends, Nick says he would be able to cope with any disintegration of the band.

Julian epitomises the cool and slightly errant image the band have. When so many of his music peers are detoxing, liposuction-ing, dieting and purifying, Julian enjoys a drink, smokes like a chimney and uses beer for hair gel. He swears so much he is trying to curb what he sees as a 'fucking' bad habit by using 'freakin'' as a parent-friendly substitute.

Drugs often rear their head with young bands in the midst of a whirlwind album-tour-album-tour schedule. Pressured by performing to great expectations each night but exhausted by the relentless schedules, hundreds of promising bands have dabbled with drugs socially or to stay awake, but with catastrophic effects. Although The Strokes have never denied using softer drugs in various forms, they are acutely aware of how rock's past is littered with the corpses of those who have succumbed in this way. The Strokes arrived in 2001 armed with an archival knowledge of music history which seems to have equipped them well for avoiding the more dangerous perils of celebratory burn-out.

"EVERY TIME WE PLAY I FEEL LIKE KISSING EVERYONE IN THE CROWD AND GOING HOME AND PARTYING WITH THEM"

The band have a 'no girlfriends' policy on the road, a mutually agreed core commandment to avoid the revolving-door affairs that have split so many groups in the past. "They distract you," explains Nikolai. "They make you think of other things than music. You can have girlfriends at home, but on tour it creates a weird atmosphere." Fab has a girlfriend of three years and enjoys staying faithful while other members of the band enjoy the pleasures that casual female companionship can bring to life on the road. Fab enjoys speculating over potential situations that arise, laying mental odds on who will and who won't and who with. Albert is brutally frank about the groupie world: "There are definitely nights when you can't get laid and there are nights when you have too many options. I usually hold off until I'm at least sure that she wouldn't mind making out with me."

It is perhaps safe to say that unless they have mentioned it previously in the evening, the gaggle of girls chatting away and sharing a drink with the band into the small hours are unlikely to converse about the merits of playing a Rickenbacker 12-string over a Les Paul gold top. Some female fans, however, do indeed have more honourable intentions — one Japanese girl spent all day trying to get through to the band in their hotel and, on finally succeeding, she presented them with a pair of socks each and a pot of home made pasta.

AFTER the triumphant Reading show, The Strokes flew up to Scotland for T In The Park in a country which they have repeatedly eulogised as having the most amazing crowds (and according to Albert, the best beer). A gig at Liverpool's Lomax was then squeezed in before they flew straight back to the USA, plunging headlong into a series of nearly 40 North American shows between then and the New Year. Amongst the notable on this US tour included The Fillmore in San Francisco, the Hammerstein Ballroom in New York and two shows to close the tour at the end of 2001 at the famous Apollo Theater, in New York's Harlem district.

Halfway through this latest set of gruelling shows, the band showed their generous side by extending their soundcheck at Birdy's in Indianapolis for a 15-year-old girl who was desperate to see them, but was unable to attend that night's over-21s-only show. The Strokes were still on the crest of a wave and loving every minute: "Every time we play I feel like kissing everyone in the crowd and going home and partying with them," Fab raved. "There's just a vibe in the room, an energy."

THE Strokes had started recording their début album before they even had a record deal in America. Although they were being courted by dozens of native labels, they were confident enough of their own material to begin the sessions with only Rough Trade officially on board. For a major record company, it is highly unusual for an unsigned band to come to the negotiating table with an album already underway, but such was the media interest in The Strokes that the prospective deals on offer were not affected at all.

In a nod to the expectant public and media cynics, the album was to be called *Is This It*. It was recorded at the same Transporter Raum Studio owned by Gordon Raphael where they had captured that very first demo.

On the suggestion of Geoff Travis, initial sessions had been started with the noted producer Gil Norton, famed for his work with The Pixies and Hüsker Dü. The band met over breakfast with Norton and requested that he didn't make them sound "like the Foo Fighters" and although all six of them got on well, The Strokes were not comfortable with the results. "It ended up sounding like a bad version of us. It didn't sound like we ever sound… too clean and that made parts sound too pretentious… like we were trying too hard." Three songs were recorded but never used. Reverting to the location and chemistry

that had worked so well for their scorching demo tape, The Strokes once again shared production duties with the amiable Gordon Raphael. Fab was very clear why Raphael was their ideal choice: "I really love the way Gordon and The Strokes do their thing. We're a good team. He doesn't have an ego. We are so incredibly lucky in that I think that all the people we have worked with, including Gordon, have let us happen."

During the six weeks of exhaustive sessions, the emphasis was very much on the band's instinctively gritty sound. According to *NME*, the studio itself was in the perfect location, deep down in the bowels of the Big Apple, past staircases of rusting radiators and graffiti-covered doors. Candles were lit and placed around the studio and the walls had red glitter on them. *Star Trek* posters competed with pictures of John Lennon and the American flag. The air was thick with cigarette smoke and pictures of lingerie-clad models from a

"PICTURE THE BAND COMING IN, RECORDING THE SONG ONCE AND THEN LEAVING. I LIKE THE IDEA OF THAT RAW EFFICIENCY"

Victoria's Secret catalogue were taped to a speaker cabinet. "This is where The Strokes hang out," reported *NME*'s man on the spot. "The room's dingy, lit by a few perfunctory lights and bare apart from a red velvet sofa with an enormous split down the middle. There's a chandelier hanging lifelessly from the ceiling, and through the glass partition we can make out three figures, one of whom is Julian (who's got his head in his hands)." Technically, however, the studio itself was far from back-to-basics, with all-digital to ProTools hardware, a deceptively advanced set-up.

The Strokes played many of the elements of the songs live, as a band, and Raphael said this made them "really demanding of their instrumentation". Nick explained how they insisted on keeping studio work simple: "The way people record things these days, and the way things are produced… things sound like bullshit."

JP Bowersock, their guitar teacher and mentor, was pivotal in the genesis of the album, an almost constant presence in the long and tiring sessions. Both Strokes guitarists looked to him for feedback and advice, while Julian was constantly bouncing ideas off him. As Nick later recalled, "There was never a time when we were there that he wasn't there. Even if we stayed until seven in the morning, he stayed to seven in the morning... he was articulating things to the producer that we couldn't articulate."

For a band so fixed in their vision and goal, it is a credit to The Strokes that they were eager to acknowledge JP's role, printing a picture of him and naming him as 'Guru' on the sleevenotes for *Is This It*. The arty mugshots of each band member were complemented by two more key personnel, Gordon Raphael and Ryan Gentles, listed as 'Wiz Kid'.

Julian found the sessions very draining, often getting little more than four hours sleep a night. For Albert, there were more pressing practical, or rather physical repercussions of playing so much guitar – severe blisters. His fingers became so sore that he resorted to the famed Stevie Ray Vaughan trick of super-gluing his fingertips onto his forearm and then ripping the skin off. The theory was that the extra layer of skin provided a comforting buffer between the sores and the strings.

Nevertheless the band thrived in these demanding circumstances, and found their bedraggled bodies and mental weariness added extra edge to the fruitful sessions. Averse to being credited as co-producers, Julian preferred instead to "picture the band coming in, recording the song once and then leaving. I like the idea of that raw efficiency". He also told *NME* that... "Recording sucks your soul. I swear to God I've never wanted a vacation as much as I do now. I mean, it's fun... but the pressure is insurmountable." Often, after a session, the band would retire to a bar called 2A, which was only half a block from the studio, where they would invariably talk into the new dawn about their recordings-in-progress.

They knew that what they were doing would always haunt them if they did not get things right. "It was the first time we went into a studio for an album," said Albert, "and we were just trying our best. A studio is such a weird place. You're playing music and you're trying to capture it onto a tape that is going to last forever which you can't change."

With the album in the can, The Strokes retired to their New York apartments to prepare themselves for the September 2001 release in the UK.

CHAPTER NINE

"BEING A 24 HOUR SODDING ICON IS HARD WORK. BEING IN BARS ALL DAY, GETTING NO SLEEP AND TRYING TO LOOK SEXY ALL THE TIME"

IAN McCULLOCH

AMONG the many rumours and tales surrounding The Strokes was the myth that they were constantly getting involved in fights, either amongst themselves or with others. During the period when they submitted themselves for their first *NME* interview/feature in New York, they were at one point taunted by a passing crowd of youths, whereupon they sprang to their own defence, first with the middle finger salute, then with fists flying. The altercation was stopped only after the intervention of the NYPD. Declining to press charges against the baying youths, The Strokes had nonetheless inadvertently secured themselves a reputation as street fighting men. This was not helped by reports that Nick and Fab would often lunge into a crowd to accost tiresome hecklers.

Julian has dismissed such behaviour as the natural consequence of living in New York, suggesting that the oppressive nature of the city is what gives their music such an edge and which occasionally overspills. "I love New York," he says. "The only thing is, when you're here, you constantly feel like you've got to get out. Human evolution didn't mean for people to be in a city like this all the time. You get so fucking aggressive about everything. You want to fight all the time, because you're so pissed off with people living on top of you."

This aggressive stance was an early press angle on the band, a situation exacerbated when a UK press officer acknowledged that he rarely visits New York without having to mediate some brawl or other. The Strokes quickly moved to dilute such talk, as Albert explains: "We don't fight. I've tried to get rid of that rumour. It's not a good one to have. If you punch someone, nothing changes." The problem was, this *NME* piece was their first major music press coverage and the stereotype of a harsh, fighting, brawling, punky NY guitar band fitted perfectly. "We get in a few fights, but there's more to it than that... really, we're just five mates making music and having a good time."

Paradoxically, much has been made of The Strokes predilection for hugging – and even kissing – each other. Indeed, their tactile demeanour in interviews even led to some comical 'gay' rumours. They do not hide the fact they kiss each other, but put it down to brotherly camaraderie rather than sexual intimacy. Fab, the joker in the pack, was happy to elaborate on this thorny issue when he said: "It's not a regular thing. But we're that comfortable with each other, we're that close to each other; the boundaries that society has set saying 'this is what a friend does and this is what a lover does' is a little skewed when it comes to The Strokes. We're not homosexual." Detractors just snorted at what they saw as another cynical ploy to grab cheap headlines.

"WE DON'T FIGHT. I'VE TRIED TO GET RID OF THAT RUMOUR. IT'S NOT A GOOD ONE TO HAVE"

HEADLINES seemed to follow The Strokes everywhere. Of all the bands to whom they have been compared, their press profile and early career heavily mirrors one recent classic UK act – Oasis. The arrival of Oasis was much the same as that of The Strokes. The Gallagher brothers, like Julian, came from a broken family, their mother Margaret bringing them up after having split up with their sometime country-and-western DJ father. Living on the polar opposite side of life to Julian's father, on a grim Manchester estate in Burnage, Noel and Liam were fired up by The Smiths, The Stone Roses and even punk before eventually fell into a band together. After Creation Records boss Alan McGee went to see a gig by 18 Wheeler but arrived early and caught the support act, Oasis, he reportedly offered them a record contract on the spot.

Like Guns N' Roses before them and The Strokes after them, Oasis were a gang. MTV loved them all and made them stars. The music press were quick to spot their musical potential, but they also glorified the in-fighting within the band, especially between the two Gallagher brothers. Such headlines were a powerful but secondary foundation for a career that turned Oasis into one of Britain's biggest ever rock acts. Between April 1994 and March 1996, they recorded as fine a sequences of singles ever released in the UK: 'Supersonic', 'Shakermaker', 'Live Forever', 'Cigarettes And Alcohol', 'Whatever', 'Some Might Say', 'Roll With It', 'Wonderwall' and 'Don't Look Back In Anger'. These songs had the uncanny ability to sound fresh yet feel like an instant classic at the same time. There was a period between 1993 and 1996 when all that the Gallagher brothers touched turned to gold.

Alongside the fights, the tabloid frenzy, the classic singles and raucous tour tales, Oasis always emanated an iconic image, most famously captured by Jill Furmanovksy's stunning black and white photographs and the cleverly designed record sleeve artwork. Liam was the epitome of what a rock frontman should look like.

Their open homage to The Beatles did not dilute their impact, although some critics felt this overly referential approach started to falter as the Nineties wore on. Nonetheless, their debut album, *Definitely Maybe* and its successor *(What's The Story) Morning Glory?* are recognised as watershed moments in British rock. Noel, like Julian, always had a very acute and focussed vision of exactly where his band was heading and the precise execution of that masterplan appears, on reflection, never to have been in doubt. Even when

Oasis, like The Strokes, were interviewed larking around and fighting with each other, their intense ambition was always apparent. Whether The Strokes will surpass – or even equal – the impact of Oasis remains to be seen. However, in a world weary of nu-metal and pop idols, the Strokes' arrival was the first breath of fresh rock air since the Manchester rock gods' halcyon days.

OPENING with the sound of a tape fast forwarding, The Strokes' début album *Is This It* dives straight into a simple, metronomic drum line, so typical of much of Fab's rhythm work. The album's title track is perhaps the band's softest song, the closest they get to a ballad. Nikolai's jaunty bass line is an odd yet complementary companion to the melancholic vocals and resigned guitars. There is none of the wild distortion and whiplash snarl of their more brutal tracks. Julian's vocals are tangibly weary; you can almost feel his exhaustion.

The tempo is immediately ramped up with the track that started it all, 'The Modern Age', re-recorded for this album (as was 'Barely Legal' and 'Last Nite', much to the dismay of some hardcore Strokes fans). Next track 'Soma' smacks of the jerky rhythms of Talking Heads, starting and ending with identical guitar/drum chimes. The robotic, snappy drum beats again drive the track, filled with juicy hook lines and memorably simple guitar riffs throughout. Velvet Underground were rarely this buoyant, except perhaps for 'Rock And Roll'. At times Julian's passionate but treated vocals edge close to Bono's similarly effected voice on U2's 'dance' albums, *Achtung Baby* and *Zooropa*.

After the foot-tapping buzz of 'Barely Legal' raises the ante again, the band evoke memories of Johnny Marr-inspired greatness with the beautiful 'Someday'. This romanticism is introduced with a shuffling, almost rockabilly sensibility, seamlessly segued into the Smiths-like chorus. Julian's vocals always verge on the sneering, but here there is enough exuberance to keep the mood decidedly upbeat. The bass and drum break contrast nicely with the interlocking and frantic rhythm guitar lines of Albert and Nick, whose teamwork on this album is one of The Strokes' single biggest strengths.

Then The Strokes lurch straight back to New York circa the Seventies for a track which opens with lyrical hints of cunnilingus, 'Alone, Together'. Rammed full with angular power riffs and a whirl of alternating-notes, the track's staccato rhythm reminds the listener of classic era Buzzcocks, especially 'Harmony In The Head'. The climactic guitar solo is merely an extended rhythm barrage, rising to a swirling pinnacle before reaching its close with a repeat of the central guitar hook. A perfectly crafted track, 'Alone, Together' is also the name of The Strokes' official fan club.

Next up is the re-recording of the modern classic 'Last Nite', then the second single 'Hard To Explain', paired here with its former companion, 'New York City Cops'. The howls at the start of this track are a good example of the ad-libbing extras the band spliced onto the album. Julian enjoyed himself by introducing each track or take with a comic line, perhaps a pub singer or a cabaret introduction for the "Ladeez in the audience". One such feral yelp was meant as a pastiche of Aerosmith which was subsequently used as the perfect intro to 'New York City Cops'.

The tempo was pulled down to the album's mellowest point with the penultimate song, 'Trying Your Luck', an often overlooked slice of classic disjointed pop. Once again, Julian's melancholic vocals sit perfectly with the brooding, stabbing guitars. Finally, 'Take It Or Leave It' closes this breath-taking début album with another example of buzzsaw guitars and machine gun drums. The interplay between Nick and Albert is again a deftly woven team effort, climaxing in reckless and wild sonic abandonment, joined at the finale by Julian's raucous, barking voice. This was the sole track where Albert used the bridge pickup of his trusty Fender Stratocaster; elsewhere, his loyalties were clear: "That middle pickup is the one man, it just matches with everything I want to do. Every now and again, I think about getting a new guitar and the others tell me that I can't - and I have to agree."

The title of the album deliberately leaves off the grammatically correct question mark ("Aesthetically it didn't look right") and featured on the cover sleeve a photo of a woman's bare legs and buttocks, with a leather-clad glove resting on the crest of a cheek. There was a whiff of Helmut Newton about the image, with its stark lines and suggestive curves. Some speculated that the posterior belonged to a member of the band, others that it was another man or maybe even a mannequin. Observers pointed out the resemblance to the concept of the famous Spinal Tap album, *Smell The Glove*, but the band had a more mundane explanation: "The cover picture was taken by the same guy who had taken the pictures for the inside cover, Colin Lane. It was just a photograph he took of his girlfriend, so it was really, really nice of him to let us use it." In America, the artwork was altered for fear of upsetting that country's notoriously conservative retail industry and right-wing lobby.

Then it was all over, a breathless 36 minutes after it had begun. Such unusual brevity, reminiscent of the Ramoes, was part of its appeal. *Is This It* was a finely crafted, achingly infectious début. Maybe it will not 'save rock'n'roll' but then the band never suggested it would. For now, The Strokes had delivered on their early promise. The best début album since Oasis? Definitely… maybe.

CHAPTER TEN

"I KNOW IT'S A LOVE-HATE THING. THERE ARE PEOPLE THAT ARE BIG FANS AND PEOPLE THAT HATE ME"

AXL ROSE

THE band made no secret of the fact they loved their album, critics were falling over themselves to review it as the year's best, and it just remained to see if the public agreed. Fab was keen for record-buyers to see beyond the hype: "It's so easy for people to jump to the wrong conclusions when they've only heard (a few songs). While we are really appreciative of some of the comparisons we have been given, it is not the full picture. Hopefully when the album comes out people will realise it isn't just some New York thing and that it is a lot more universal than that."

In the UK, it entered the album charts at number two, and it was perhaps a little disappointing that it failed to top the list immediately after so much frenzied media attention. Ironically, for a band touted as the perfect antidote to nu-metal's dated machismo, the widely berated metal heads Staind kept New York's finest off the top spot.

By year's end, *Is This It* had easily scooped the *NME*'s 'Album of the Year' award, ahead of Spiritualized's *Let It Come Down*, The White Stripes' *White Blood Cells*, Jay Z's *The Blueprint*, and Starsailor's *Love Is Here*. They also won 'Best New Act' and 'Band of the Year'. They secured *Rolling Stone*'s eighth best 'Album of the Year' but managed to grab the top spot for similar polls in *Time*, *New York Magazine* and *Entertainment Weekly*.

There were, of course, the occasional dissenters, such as this rather funny and brave overview in an insightful article by Ned Raggett in *Freaky Trigger* magazine: "Casablancas and his merry men provoke little to no reaction from me, the music congealing slowly like globs of drying paint on a hot but humid day, unremarkably trundling along… you just sort of stare at it, at least if you're me, and think, 'Huh. Well, okay'… The real problem with the Strokes is that of all the recent boy bands, they're the most singularly uninteresting."

Nonetheless, momentum in the UK could not have been higher, but despite generally encouraging reviews in the American media, The Strokes profile in their homeland was far more modest than in Britain. Like Bush in reverse, for a while they could not leave a venue in the UK without being besieged by fans, while at home, few kids even recognised them. Fab was only recognised in his local drum shop as late as autumn 2002. Even then, the sales assistant apologised, saying he'd only heard "the song with the drum machine on".

"NEW YORK IS MEANT TO BE CLEANED UP, BUT IT'S GETTING TENSER AGAIN. LATELY, WHEN I'M WALKING AROUND THE STREET, I REALLY FEEL IT."

The gulf between US indifference and UK adoration is not lost on the band, but they seem happy enough to allow their domestic profile to grow more organically. They have suggested, probably accurately, that a greater proportion of UK rock fans are intent on seeking out new music while their American counterparts seem satisfied with the familiar. The challenge facing The Strokes in America far surpasses that in the UK. It is unlikely that they will strike an emotional chord with an angst-filled teenager in the Midwest or the sparsely populated towns of the deep south, where the fawning of the fashion cognoscenti and celebrity admirers means nothing. Some observers insist the band's production puritanism will cost them dearly in the rush for radio play in a nation where super-production and airwave gloss is king. The Strokes' next big challenge, like every aspiring major band before them, will be to take their music to these disparate and hard-to-crack corners of the United States. Can they succeed? That remains to be seen.

Circumstances beyond geography and momentum conspired to stall The Strokes' progress in America. The terrorist atrocities of September 11th, 2001, saw the release of their début album in America put back to early October. Entirely of their own volition, The Strokes tactfully decided to remove the track 'New York City Cops' out of respect and deference to the force which had lost so many of its men when the World Trade Center towers collapsed. Instead, the band recorded and spliced in the somewhat less impressive 'When It Started', but the gesture was admirable nonetheless.

'New York City Cops' was not actually a slight on that city's police force. The lead lyric "they ain't too smart" was merely the wording which Julian preferred best, having also considered New York City Girls, New York City Clubs and even New York City Cocks. The song itself was actually just about girls. "I just thought we'd try to do something positive," he said. The song, one of their fans' live favourites, was also removed from any live shows the band played in that city.

Interestingly, The Strokes' friends The Moldy Peaches actually had a track already released on their own album which was unintentionally far more directly entwined with the awful events of September 11. Unable to withdraw the track as the album had already been shipped to stores, the song was called 'NYC's Like A Graveyard'. It was actually a harsh indictment of the city's posing scenesters, but with images of bodies walking the streets and lyrics such as "all the tombstones skyscrapin'", its timing could not have been more unfortunate. Gladly The Moldy Peaches did not suffer any criticism for this track, which was issued in all innocence.

With the rubble on Ground Zero being cleared up and the emotional damage only just beginning to manifest itself, Julian suggested these terrible events had raised tension in the city, drawing comparisons with the violent period before Mayor Rudolph Gulliano's era of zero tolerance, when the Big Apple was the murder capital of the world. "New York is meant to be cleaned up, but it's getting tenser again. Lately, when I'm walking around the street, I really feel it."

The band had all been in New York in preparation for the album's launch when the two airplanes slammed into the World Trade Center towers, so the events of 9-11 are marked indelibly in their minds, just like every other New Yorker that day. Nikolai was alerted to events by a worried phone call from his step-grandmother. "All you could do was what everyone in New York was doing - looking either out their windows or at their TVs in utter disbelief.

RECEIVING 'BEST INTERNATIONAL NEWCOMER' AWARD AT THE BRITS

For a few days afterward, New York was very strange. There was this bizarre uncertainty. All anybody could do was just wait it out."

The Strokes were happy to help when asked to play at the Beastie Boys concert to raise funds for victims of 9-11. The shows, held at the city's Hammerstein Ballroom and featuring other acts such as Jon Spencer Blues Explosion and The Roots, also saw unexpected appearances from Moby, Bono and Michael Stipe. In excess of $125,000 was raised.

WITHIN a matter of weeks of its release, *Is This It* had sold over one million copies worldwide, edging nearer to two million by the end of 2002. Maybe this isn't all that impressive when you consider that Eminem sold more than two million in one week with *The Eminem Show*. However, The Strokes know that America is yet to fall under its spell in quite the same way the UK did. In the USA, they were initially selling 15,000 copies a week, a modest but encouraging start. This saw the album enter the *Billboard* charts at number 74. Following a January 2002 performance on *Saturday Night Live*, sales of *Is This It* doubled to 40,000 a week for some time, taking the record up to a chart peak of the low 30s. Gold status was achieved on the way to a mid-2002 US total of 400,000 units, which in the wake of September 11th and the nation's predilection for 'comforting' music, was commendable if not spectacular. The band still have a long, long way to go to be ranked alongside Slim Shady as one of the truly global acts – after all, Eminem's riotous and acerbic music is not renowned for being 'comforting' but that didn't stop him releasing yet another multi-million selling international number one album.

The Strokes boosted sales of the album by the release of their third UK single, 'Last Nite' in November 2001. This track was perhaps their closest homage to The Stooges, being particularly akin to 'Lust For Life'. There was a little disappointment that the band chose to re-release a track that had originally been on that first demo tape, but this did not stop the record charting at number fourteen. This time it came with a deliberately low budget video, directed by Roman Coppola, which perfectly captured their gritty urban personae. On a more jovial note, The Strokes performed a 'secret' gig at the Mercury Lounge in January 2002 under the pseudonym of The Shitty Beatles.

Acclaim for the album and early releases lasted well into the New Year. In February 2002, The Strokes received the 'Best International Newcomer' Award at the Brits in Earl's Court, London. Perhaps predictably, they were not too overawed: "I don't think it means much at all," said Nick. "I don't think it's any gauge of how good your music is. Getting a platinum disc meant more to us because it meant a certain amount of people own our album, listen to it and have it in their CD collection." They were also nominated in the 'Best International Act' category (won by Destiny's Child) and in the 'Best International Album' category (scooped by Kylie Minogue). They also performed 'Last Nite' live with a Union Jack draped from the corner of the stage.

The following month, their predominance in the UK market was confirmed with two sell-out shows at the 4,000 capacity Brixton Academy. This was surprisingly early for a band at this stage in their career, but perfectly reflected the haste which had shadowed The Strokes throughout their rise to fame. One of the hottest shows of the year, all 8,000 seats sold in just 45 minutes and touts were busy selling tickets outside for £150. Spring 2002 saw the release of 'The Modern Age' in the UK and Europe, much to the dismay of some fans who thought they had mined the album too much already. At least there was some new material with the inclusion of 'When It Started' on the soundtrack for the year's biggest film, *Spider-man*. The OST also featured Aerosmith, Sum 41 and The Hives.

In the glare of the media publicity swirling around The Strokes, it is easy to ignore the fact that here was a young band that was gigging *very* hard. During the year they played just shy of 100 shows, including over 50 in the USA to predominantly smaller audiences, plus half that amount to an already converted UK (forcing them to fly in the face of their band motto of "Never board a plane if you think there's something wrong with the engine"). They also visited

Australasia for eleven shows, as well as a début European tour, plus gigs in Japan and Canada. Their critics may have still seen them as little more than pretty boys with large wallets, but being workshy was certainly not an charge you could level at them with any credence. The sheer volume of shows saw them grow in composed confidence, replacing their initial stage fright with a formidable live force.

Another point worth remembering is that for large parts of this early phase, they had only 15 active songs. They often performed the songs from their début album from start to finish in sequential order. Around the start of 2002, they had the luxury of a few more tracks, but would still work out their set list each night by saying "It's 11 out of 15". The eleven songs on the UK version of *Is This It* were complemented by 'When It Started', the song which replaced 'New York City Cops' on the US version of the début album. Then they also had three new songs, namely 'The Way It Is', 'Meet Me In The Bathroom' (which Julian denied was inspired by Courtney Love) and the jokingly titled 'Ze Newie'. Actually, this song was christened in the media by mistake after The Strokes performed it at a German festival and Julian light-heartedly introduced it as such. The song was first played at a New Year's Eve show at the Apollo in New York, having been written just six weeks before. 'Meet Me In The Bathroom' was also first composed around this time and Albert was confident of its calibre: "I think it's a good song, it's a mixture of rock and something that is so melodic because the chord progression is an old jazz chord progression from the Twenties."

WEEZER

The Strokes seemingly unstoppable tour did temporarily crash to a sudden halt in early July 2002 when Julian seriously injured his knee. He was at a barbecue in Los Angeles with friends, when he and Fab began play fighting and in the resulting melée, Julian managed to sustain a serious cartilage trauma. As a result of the damage, three dates on a tour supporting Weezer - in Cleveland, Indianapolis and Columbus - had to be cancelled. The band had enjoyed these shows even though Nick evidently lost his girlfriend to a member of Weezer! With an almost comic philosophical resignation, Nick said, "Man, you cannot not like Weezer. I still like Weezer."

In the aftermath of these cancellations, the band did receive many angry letters from disappointed fans but were back on the road again as quickly as Julian's doctors would permit. His first show back after the injury was at a disused gothic church gig in Pontiac by the name of Clutch Cargo, which was part of a series of dates co-headlining with The White Stripes. Along with The Strokes, this American act was considered to be at the forefront of a garage rock revival.

The band had befriended the critically lauded White Stripes – another *NME* favourite – after a period of mutual admiration. The Strokes had first seen

THE WHITE STRIPES

The White Stripes when the latter played a four night residency at The Bowery in New York. In August 2002, the two acts played this series of co-headlining shows in America to frantic crowds. The show at Radio City Music Hall on August, 15 was in front of 6,000 fans, their biggest non-festival show in the USA to date. Beck was in the audience to see Jack from The White Stripes join them on stage for 'New York City Cops' and later, when

The Strokes were finished, Julian introduced the Stripes by saying, "Enjoy your next band, I've forgotten what they're fucking called."

At these and numerous other dates to follow, Julian performed all the set from a stool. Even the harshest Strokes critic would have had to have felt sorry for him when one night he dropped the mike and was fumbling around in obvious pain trying to recover it from the stage midway through 'Hard To Explain'. Jack from the White Stripes cheered him on for this first show back by shouting "Break a leg!"

THE rush of fame, touring and acclaim have certainly unsettled the band at times, as Julian said, "I guess I'm confused between everything I thought when we started and everything I think now." He added,

"I never had the rock-star dream. I thought it would be cool to be a modern-day composer."

In interviews they were occasionally quoted as complaining about the rigours of touring, denying rumours that Julian hit a French record company executive after a row and bemoaning the various record company obligations they have – such as store signings, radio tours and filming promo videos. It seems unduly early in the gruelling album-tour-album-tour-burnout treadmill for The Strokes to be complaining, but in their defence this is entirely in keeping with the time-warp speed of their career to date, which seems to have condensed rock'n'roll's various career stages into a matter of months.

One complaint that many young bands air is that as their crowds increase, any sense of intimacy fades. The Strokes feel the opposite. "When we first came over (to the UK), there was a sense that a lot of people were there because it was cool to see us, not 'cos they liked us. As we're playing to larger crowds, the real fans are able to get in easier."

"I NEVER HAD THE ROCK-STAR DREAM. I THOUGHT IT WOULD BE COOL TO BE A MODERN-DAY COMPOSER"

When The Strokes had first appeared on the UK music scene, many people had noted how amenable they were in interviews and how their stylish image and designer dress sense seemed to belie a distinctly approachable demeanour. The 'best band in the world' tag did not appear to have affected their natural bonhomie at all. Nevertheless, by the end of 2002 the band, and in particular Julian, were much more guarded in interviews, no less amicable but more aware of the Pandora's box that is the media.

They have made mistakes. For one TV show in Paris they had a disagreement with their record company for that territory and did not play the show. Then they discovered that 50 kids had won tickets to see them perform and had taken days off school and travelled miles for the big day. With an admirable conscience that they will do well to preserve, when the band found this out they were dismayed and proceeded to phone up each and every fan to apologise. They even arranged to meet them all at a Paris bar, where they chatted and signed autographs.

CHAPTER ELEVEN

"THERE'S NOTHING WORSE THAN A WHINY MUSICIAN. MAKE YOUR WORK, STAY COMMITTED TO YOUR WORK, STAND BY YOUR WORK AND SHUT UP"

TORI AMOS

IN the aftermath of their hit album, Julian and Albert moved into a shared flat near to Greenwich Village. The 'H'-shaped apartment enables each of them to live at one end, with a communal kitchen in the centre. While Albert is always meticulously tidy, Julian is the opposite but this doesn't lead to strife as they have their own separate spaces. Being such close mates, they often roll in after a night on the town and crash into whichever bed they reach first. More recently, Albert admits that since Julian's girlfriend moved in, they try to stay out of the same bed as otherwise it would be "a bit weird". One reporter noted that their fridge contained nothing but four bottles of cider and a jar of peanut butter. Over Albert's bed hangs an oil painting of a reclining lady painted by Fab (who is also a sculptor). The Strokes drummer had been living with his mother while their career had been taking off, but then moved in with a girlfriend and band manager Ryan Gentles. Nikolai might soon be welcoming Nick into his home after his girlfriend had left him for the aforementioned member of Weezer.

Inevitably with such superstar fans, The Strokes have started mixing in celebrity circles. Perhaps the highest profile friendship has been the rumoured romance between Hollywood actress Drew Barrymore (*ET*, *Charlie's Angels*) and Fab. He would not be drawn on this in numerous interviews, saying only that "she is one of the most perfect people I've ever met". News that The Strokes will support The Rolling Stones on two dates in October 2002 only confirms just how high their star is orbiting in the celebrity universe.

Celebrities continue to flock around The Strokes. One odd spin-off of their high profile was the news that American singer/songwriter Ryan Adams had recorded an acoustic cover of the entire *Is This It* album. Albert was desperate to hear the tracks, saying, "That's so cool. I'd love to hear it. That's rad, man. We hang out together in a bar in New York sometimes. He's cool." Elsewhere, The Strokes were already soliciting a rash of wannabee copyists. One major UK record company A&R man complained in mid-2002 that every time he ventured into Camden to see a potential new signing he was "confronted by a stage filled with greasy haired, DKNY rejects, trying to look like models and sound like Lou Reed but actually looking like Paul Calf in a cheap leather jacket." The Strokes imitations have even manifested themselves on record in the shape of *The Different Strokes EP* by a band of the same name, which is a UK cover album of Strokes songs played note for note on a toy organ. A bootleg remix of 'Hard To Explain' spliced with Christina Aguilera's 'Genie In A Bottle' was also released under the name of 'Stroke Of Genius' and quickly proved very popular in UK clubs.

"THERE'S NO POINT IN MAKING COOL MUSIC IF NO ONE'S GOING TO HEAR IT."

THE problem for The Strokes may well now be… how do you follow that? Julian's burning ambition demands that they move on to a better album, more acclaim and greater success. They are not drawn to obscurity: "There's no point in making cool music if no one's going to hear it." The few new songs already aired live do not suggest any loss of the sort of quality control that made *Is This It* such a pivotal record.

One of the age-old problems for a new band is finding the downtime to write the new material that everyone demands. Prolific touring has left The Strokes with very little spare time to create new songs, so they are keen to enjoy the end of 2002 away from the rigours of the road. "Touring makes a band fragile," Julian told BBC's *Planet Sound*. "It's not a healthy life, mentally or physically, if you stay on tour for too long. It's going to be some time before our next record is written. I'd estimate it would take a full year of being at home in New York to write… I can relax there, cut myself off from all the attention the band's had. The only pressure is to make our songs as good as they can be."

They are mature enough to recognise the pitfalls of over-work, particularly on the road: "We're cutting right back," he says. "From now on, we'll only play shows that look cool – a festival here and there, or countries we've not been to. I stand by our songs, same as I ever did. But there's a danger of them being over-familiar, to the band and the fans. We need to stir things up again."

The Strokes are planning to work on sessions for the second album in late 2002/early 2003, although the pressure they constantly thrust upon themselves is already mounting. A new song is not classified as such until "it is better than

AT THE 2002 MTV VIDEO MUSIC AWARDS

the current ones". Julian knows that the public and media expectations for this new record will be staggering and is trying to not become daunted by that prospect: "If you don't do anything that's better, it's not very exciting. I think a lot of people have faith in us but they're not completely sure because they've only heard one record."

He also said, "I feel like we will experiment more when we're more experienced. When we're better players, we'll have more knowledge of the actual buttons. I also think we might be able to work faster." Fab Moretti was even blunter: "I think what we've done isn't much yet. Hopefully, we'll have a future ahead of us. I know we are not the best band we can possibly be.

We all have to work harder. The moment we start thinking we are the best band on the block is the very moment that we pigeonhole ourselves and fuck up. If anything, we've just opened a door."

Rough Trade are surprisingly supportive of this more considered approach to the new material: "We don't want The Strokes to milk their fame," said Geoff Travis. "We want them to go and write some new songs. We want them to make records for as long as they want to make records. I'm looking forward to the third, fourth and fifth albums. I hope that some of the mistakes that happen to bands like The Stone Roses don't happen to them and that we can help them to avoid falling into some of those traps."

For their own part, The Strokes swerve from modest denials of their mooted potential to outright declarations of pride at their career thus far: "I'm doing what I really wanted to do all my life and it's being executed perfectly. We talk about it all the time. It's almost too good to be true." Albert was even more buoyant: "One new song is the fucking future of rock'n'roll, man!"

Until they have the new material ready, The Strokes have to fall back on relying on *Is This It*. In September 2002, they released 'Someday' in most territories of the world. The B-sides were scheduled to be home recording versions of 'Alone, Together' and 'Is This It' recorded on a 4-track studio in one of their apartments. The video, filmed in The Powerhouse Bar in Hollywood, was again directed by Roman Coppola and featured guest appearances by Guns N' Roses and Guided By Voices. This release was final proof, if any was needed, that The Strokes were in desperate need of new material.

WHILE they are writing and recording their new album, there are scores of bands out there who are threatening to compete with them. A collection of disparate bands with a back-to-basics guitar focus – virtually all beginning with the word 'the' – have arrived to up the ante for any new Strokes songs. Although they have all been clumsily lumped together, there are signs that The Strokes will not have it all their own way on their return unless they can match the frightening quality of their début album. If not, then bands such as The White Stripes, The Vines, The Hives, The Coral, The Libertines and The Black Rebel Motorcycle Club will no doubt gladly jump into the fray. The Strokes are rightly viewed as superior to these acts at present, and may well be the best US band since Nirvana, but until they extend their impact – which they show every signs of doing thus far – *Is This It* will forever remain a definite tier below *Nevermind*. At the same time, critics who claim The Strokes must first deliver three or four albums of classic material before they can deserve to be mentioned in the same breath as Oasis, Nirvana and Velvet Underground for example, would perhaps do well to review the one album seismic impact of The Sex Pistols. For now, The Strokes' début album has temporarily sated the ravenous demand for quality music that such a cacophonous media blitz creates.

WATCHING The Strokes' rise to fame has been like watching the entire career of a rock'n'roll band crammed into a few short months. But perhaps therein lies much of the attraction – in a world of soundbites and high speed access, The Strokes are the quintessential rock'n'roll band for the modern age. The key to their healthy survival is not to avoid living their life at warp speed, which seems unavoidable, but rather to make sure they

do so with quality songs delivered with style. "It does seem a bit fast," admitted Nikolai, "but we didn't skip any levels. That's the secret of doing it. It's about working really hard and making like no effort was put into it."

Julian, an ideal frontman who can mix outright sex appeal with endearing vulnerability, has more noble ambitions: "I want to be one of those people, be they writers, poets, musicians, who leaves clues for the next generation. The really good people leave clues that help feed the human race. That's my aspiration."

EPILOGUE

ECHOING Kurt Cobain's infamous entrance in a wheelchair in 1992, Julian hobbled on stage at Reading 2002 on his crutches, getting only halfway to his microphone before throwing them aside and launching into a wild rendition of 'The Way It Is'. The four new songs slipped seamlessly into the set, as popular as the previously released Strokes' songs with the muddied thousands.

Their bill that day had been one of the best festival line-ups for years: Pulp, Weezer, Jane's Addiction, The White Stripes, The Moldy Peaches, Mercury Rev, The Breeders and Feeder. Such lofty company didn't seem to phase The Strokes at all, who finally seemed to have thrown off the last vestiges of their stage nerves.

By show's end, a frustrated Julian has toppled off his stool and sings savagely on all fours. Then, with the audience rapt, the band bring on a birthday cake for Julian, tempering their live noise temporarily before smashing straight back into a triumphant 'New York City Cops'. The tempo is ratcheted up one more notch with the mid-song appearance of Jack from The White Stripes, who accompanies The Strokes. But this is The Strokes' night, their month and certainly their year. The long-time fanatics at *NME* frothed that "this is the greatest gig The Strokes have ever played on UK soil". Let's hope it is not the last.

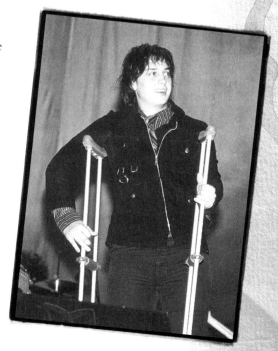

DISCOGRAPHY

SINGLES

THE MODERN AGE EP
Rough Trade Records
Released January, 2001

The Modern Age
Last Nite
Barely Legal

HARD TO EXPLAIN
Rough Trade Records
Released June, 2001

Hard To Explain
New York City Cops

LAST NITE
RCA/Rough Trade Records
Released November, 2001

CD 1
Last Nite (album version)
When It Started

CD 2:
Last Nite
Take It Or Leave It
Trying Your Luck
All tracks recorded live at KCRW Radio.

HARD TO EXPLAIN EP
RCA/Rough Trade Records
Re-released April 2002
In Ireland a 1000 copy limited edition of 'Hard To explain' was released with the following tracks:

Hard To Explain
The Modern Age
Last Nite
When It Started
Take It Or Leave It (live)

ALBUMS

IS THIS IT
Rough Trade Records
Released August, 2001

Is This It
The Modern Age
Soma
Barely Legal
Someday
Alone Together
Last Nite
Hard To Explain
New York City Cops
Trying Your Luck
Take It Or Leave It

In North America, the track 'New York City Cops' was replaced by 'When It Started'. However, the vinyl version of the album did contain 'New York City Cops'.